real food

Loukie Werle

Real Food is published jointly by
ACP Publishing Pty Ltd (ABN 18 053 273 546) and
Media 21 Publishing Pty Ltd (ABN 82 090 635 073).

ACP Publishing
54 Park Street, Sydney, NSW 2000
Tel: (02) 9282 8000

Media 21 Publishing Pty Ltd
30 Bay Street, Double Bay, NSW 2028
Tel: (02) 9362 1800 Fax: (02) 9362 9500
Email: m21@media21.com.au

The publishers gratefully acknowledge the assistance of
the National Heart Foundation of Australia in the preparation of this book and
especially the following Heart Foundation staff:
Project managers Nicola Stewart, Dianne Speakman
Nutrition expert Barbara Eden
Nutrition copy contributors Ernestine van Herwerden, Rebecca Yeoh

Author Loukie Werle
Designer Sharon McGrath
Photographer Alan Benson
Food stylist Mary Harris
Home economist and special assistant to the author Georgina Leonard
Colour reproduction Clayton Lloyd

Editorial Directors Media 21 Philip Gore, Craig Osment
Marketing Director Media 21 Stephen Balme

ACP Chief Executive Officer John Alexander
ACP Group Publisher Pat Ingram
ACP Deputy Publisher Christine Whiston
Business Manager Seymour Cohen

Printed by Phoenix Offset & Bookbuilders, Hong Kong
Distribution Random House (bookshops), tel: (02) 9954 9966
          Network (newsagents), tel: 1300 131 169

National Library of Australia Cataloguing-in-Publication entry
Werle, Loukie.
Real food : healthy, delicious, easy to prepare.
Includes index.
ISBN 1 876624 76 0.

1. Cookery. 2. Heart - Diseases - Diet therapy - Recipes.
3. Cardiovascular system - Diseases - Nutritional aspects.
I. National Heart Foundation of Australia. II. Title.
641.56311

real food

ACP

Contents

A Heart for Life

Things you can do every day

We are really pleased to present the new Heart Foundation cookbook, *Real Food*. More than ever, many of us are balancing demands on our time and trying to cut through the confusion of messages about healthy eating. The Heart Foundation has developed this cookbook in response to many requests – from individuals and families – who are looking for delicious, healthy recipes that are easy to prepare, together with practical health information.

Our overall message is that healthy eating is about enjoying a variety of foods from the different food groups, and that this doesn't mean you have to compromise on taste. This cookbook has a wide range of recipes, including healthy twists on classic favourites and some great new recipe ideas packed with taste and variety. There are also wonderful recipe influences from across the globe.

We have included tips that encourage you to substitute ingredients according to your taste, what's available in the cupboard, your budget or just to add variety to your cooking. Our nutritious recipes meet specific nutrition criteria for total fat, saturated fat, kilojoules (energy), sodium (salt), and fibre. Every recipe has an analysis of nutrients per serve. (See page 127 for an explanation.)

Real Food also includes practical heart health information, answers to commonly asked questions about food, and a recipe replacement guide for modifying recipes to include healthier ingredients.

Healthy eating and the cholesterol story

High blood cholesterol is a major risk factor for coronary heart disease. Making lifestyle changes, in particular making changes to the food you eat, is very important for reducing your blood cholesterol level and improving your heart health. Most people can reduce their blood cholesterol levels if they follow a healthy eating pattern that is low in saturated fat (the type of fat that raises blood cholesterol levels).

Which fat do I choose?

Fats in food are a mixture of three different types known as saturated, monounsaturated and polyunsaturated fats. Foods are usually grouped according to the type of fat present in the greatest amount. For example, the fat in butter is mainly saturated fat. The fat in sunflower oil is mainly polyunsaturated. The different types of fat have different effects on blood cholesterol levels.

- Saturated fats raise blood cholesterol levels. To reduce your blood cholesterol level it's important to reduce your intake of foods high in saturated fats such as fatty meats, full-fat dairy products, butter, two vegetable oils (coconut and palm oil), most deep-fried takeaways and commercially baked products such as biscuits and pastries.
- Polyunsaturated fats help lower blood cholesterol if your meals are low in saturated fat. Some oils and margarine spreads, nuts, seeds and fish contain polyunsaturated fats. Like all fats, polyunsaturated fats are high in kilojoules, so enjoy them in moderation.
- Monounsaturated fats can also help lower blood cholesterol if your meals are low in saturated fat. Some oils and margarine spreads, avocado, nuts and seeds contain monounsaturated fats. Like all fats, monounsaturated fats are high in kilojoules, so enjoy them in moderation.

Healthy food choices

It can be confusing trying to sort through often contradictory messages about which foods to eat more of and which foods to limit. The Heart Foundation has developed simple messages based on the latest scientific evidence to help prevent more confusion. Try to base your eating pattern on the following healthy eating guidelines:

- Use margarine spreads instead of butter or dairy blends.
- Use a variety of oils for cooking – some suitable choices include canola, sunflower, soybean, olive and peanut oils.
- Use salad dressings and mayonnaise made from oils such as canola, sunflower, soybean and olive.
- Choose low- or reduced-fat milk and yoghurt or "added calcium" soy beverages. Try to limit cheese and ice-cream to twice a week.
- Have fish (any type of fresh or canned) at least twice a week.
- Select lean meat (meat trimmed of fat and chicken without skin). Try to limit fatty meats, including sausages and delicatessen meats such as salami.
- Snack on plain, unsalted nuts and fresh fruit.
- Incorporate dried peas (for example, split peas), dried beans (for example, haricot beans, kidney beans), canned beans (for example, baked beans, three bean mix), or lentils into two meals a week.
- Base your meals around vegetables and grain-based foods such as breakfast cereals, bread, pasta, noodles and rice.
- Try to limit takeaway foods to once a week. Takeaway foods include pastries, pies, pizza, hamburgers and creamy pasta dishes.
- Try to limit snack foods such as potato crisps and corn crisps to once a week.

A Heart for Life

- Try to limit cakes, pastries and chocolate or creamy biscuits to once a week.
- Try to limit cholesterol-rich foods such as egg yolks and offal (for example, liver, kidney and brains).

Manage your weight

Being overweight is often associated with raised blood cholesterol levels and raised blood pressure levels, which are major risk factors for heart attack and blood vessel disease. The key to achieving and maintaining a healthy weight is to balance the kilojoules coming into your body through food and drinks with the kilojoules (energy) being used by the body through day-to-day activities and planned regular physical activity.

Sounds simple, but we all know that losing weight is not easy. You will need to make some changes to your lifestyle that you can enjoy and maintain for a lifetime.

Lowering your sodium intake

Healthy adults need less than 2300mg of sodium a day to balance the amount of fluid in the body and maintain muscle and nerve function. Excess sodium (salt) in the diet is linked to high blood pressure in some people. The main source of excess sodium is salt: both table salt and salt added to processed foods. One teaspoon of table salt alone provides 2000mg of sodium!

Enjoying a healthy eating pattern that is low in salt is one way to help control your blood pressure, or help to avoid getting high blood pressure. To reduce salt intake:

- Eat plenty of fresh fruit and vegetables.
- Choose low-salt bread and cereals.
- Avoid seasonings, processed foods and takeaway foods that are high in salt.
- Avoid adding salt in cooking or at the table.

It only takes a Tick

If you find shopping for healthier food choices confusing or you don't have the time to study food labels, look for this symbol when you shop. The Tick Program is the Heart Foundation's guide to help you make healthier food choices quickly and easily. Using the Heart Foundation Tick when you shop means that you don't have to be a nutrition expert to make healthier food choices. And because all foods with the Tick are independently tested and assessed against strict nutrition guidelines before getting the Tick, you can be sure you are making a healthier choice. Foods with the Tick are healthier choices among foods of their type. Tick foods meet strict standards for saturated fat, sodium (salt) and, where appropriate, kilojoules. Some are also higher in fibre. The Tick can be found on more than 1100 foods, so try foods with the Tick for a taste of healthier eating.

Other risk factors for heart disease

Healthy eating is only part of the picture to heart health and general wellbeing. Making lifestyle changes and following medical advice to reduce or remove risk factors over which you have some control is the best way to reduce the risk of developing heart disease, and to help prevent it getting worse if it already exists. Positive steps to a healthy heart include:

- **Be smokefree** If you smoke, call the Quitline 131 848 for advice on quitting. Quitting smoking is a particularly important step.
- **Enjoy healthy eating** Most people can reduce their blood cholesterol levels if they follow a healthy eating pattern that is low in saturated fat.
- **Be active every day** Try to include at least 30 minutes of moderate-intensity physical activity (such as brisk walking) on most, if not all, days of the week. The amount of activity can be accumulated in shorter bouts, such as three 10-minute walks.
- **Achieve and maintain a healthy body weight** Aim to achieve and maintain a healthy body weight. The keys to achieving and maintaining a healthy weight are to enjoy healthy eating and regular physical activity (see above).
- **Manage your blood pressure** Ensure that your blood pressure is normal. Managing your blood pressure is a particularly important consideration for people already with, or at higher risk of developing, coronary heart disease. If your blood pressure is high, reduce salt intake, limit alcohol to one (if you are female) or two (if you are male) drinks or less daily and follow your doctor's advice. Medication may also be required.
- **Seek help for depression and social isolation** People often ask if there is a link between "stress" and heart disease. The term "stress" has no exact meaning, so it is difficult to measure its effect on heart disease. However, it has been shown that people who experience depression, are socially isolated or do not have quality social support are at greater risk of developing coronary heart disease. For further information speak to your doctor.

If you would like more information regarding heart health, please ring Heartline, the Heart Foundation's telephone information service.
Call Heartline on 1300 36 27 87 (for the cost of a local call).

A practical guide to modifying recipes

Healthy eating is all about enjoying a variety of healthy foods, and the selection of recipes included in this cookbook will encourage you to prepare a variety of delicious meals. The good news is you don't have to throw out those old cookbooks or that great family stand-by. Just a few simple changes can reduce the saturated fat in your favourite recipes. The two steps to changing a recipe are:
• Try healthier cooking methods.
• Change ingredients by reducing, removing or using something else.

Method	Healthier cooking method
Deep-fry	Roast in the oven on a lined tray or grill tray. Food can be lightly steamed or microwaved first, and brushed with oil such as canola, sunflower, soybean or olive for crispness. Crumbed fish, chicken and oven fries can be cooked in the oven, rather than deep-fried.
Shallow-fry/saute	Stir-fry using reduced-salt stock, or oil such as canola, sunflower, soybean, olive or peanut. Try using a non-stick frying pan.
Roasting	Choose lean cuts of meat, or trim all visible fat. Place meat on a rack in a baking dish with 1 to 2cm of water. For extra flavour add herbs or wine to the water. Try brushing with a marinade to prevent the meat drying out or cover the food with a lid or aluminium foil for part of the cooking time. Roasting on a spit or rotisserie will allow fat to drip away. Brush or spray vegetables with oil such as canola, sunflower, soybean, olive or peanut and bake in a separate pan.
Casserole/stews	Trim fat off meat before cooking. Add legumes such as kidney beans, chickpeas, soybeans or lentils to add bulk and flavour. After cooking, chill the food so that any fat solidifies on the surface. Skim fat off the surface before reheating and thickening.
Ingredient	**Healthier alternative**
Milk, yoghurt, cream	Use low- or reduced-fat varieties. Use ricotta cheese whipped with a little icing sugar, fruit, or low- or reduced-fat milk as a substitute for cream.
Sour cream	Blend cottage cheese and low- or reduced-fat milk (add a little lemon juice or vinegar, if desired). Use low- or reduced-fat natural yoghurt. Use evaporated reduced-fat milk and lemon juice.
Cheese	Use smaller amounts of reduced-fat varieties. Use a little grated parmesan cheese instead of grated cheddar – it gives more flavour and less is needed. Mix grated reduced-fat cheese with oats, breadcrumbs or wheatgerm for toppings on casseroles, gratins and baked dishes.
Butter, margarine spreads	Use margarine spreads instead of butter, dairy blends, lard, copha or cooking fats. Reduced-fat or "Lite" spreads are generally not good for cooking.
Oil	Use a variety of oils for cooking. Some suitable choices include canola, sunflower, soybean, olive and peanut oils.
Mayonnaise/dressing	Use salad dressings and mayonnaise made from oils such as canola, sunflower, soybean and olive. Make your own using ingredients such as low- or reduced-fat yoghurt, buttermilk, tomato paste, balsamic or other vinegars, lemon juice, ricotta cheese, mustard and fruit pulp.
Meat/poultry	Choose lean meats. Remove fat from meat and skin from poultry before cooking. Marinate or add flavour with ingredients such as wine vinegars. Sear meat quickly to keep in juices.
Cakes/biscuits	Use margarine spreads or oil such as canola, sunflower or olive. The minimum fat required for biscuits is about 2 tablespoons per cup of flour. This will retain crispness. Choose plain sponges, yeast cakes and breads, muffins and scones, as they generally use less fat.
Pastry/savoury	Use filo pastry, brushing every three to four layers with oil such as canola, sunflower, soybean or olive, juice, egg white or low- or reduced-fat yoghurt. Use pastry made with oil such as canola, sunflower or olive.
Coconut cream/coconut milk	Use evaporated reduced-fat milk with a little coconut essence. For occasional use, try one of the reduced-fat coconut milks available. Alternatively, if you have time, soak desiccated coconut in warm low- or reduced-fat milk for 30 minutes then strain, discard the coconut and use the milk

Commonly asked questions

How does unhealthy eating affect my cholesterol?

Cholesterol is a fatty substance produced naturally by the body and found in your blood. It has many good uses but is a problem when there's too much of it in the blood. Too much cholesterol in the blood causes fatty and scar deposits to gradually build up in blood vessels, making it harder for blood to flow through. This can lead to heart attack or stroke.

Most of the total cholesterol in the blood is made up of "bad" (LDL) cholesterol. Only a small part is made up of "good" (HDL) cholesterol, which helps protect against coronary heart disease. Eating too much saturated fat is the main cause of a high blood cholesterol level.

Family history also plays a part. If close family members have high blood cholesterol, your chances are greater too.

What should my blood cholesterol level be?

This is something you need to discuss with your doctor. Generally, the lower your total blood cholesterol level the better. This is especially true for people with other risk factors for, or already with, heart disease. A total blood cholesterol of 4.5 mmol/litre is better than one of 5.5 mmol/litre.

What foods are high in cholesterol?

Dietary cholesterol is found only in animal products. Plant foods such as avocado, nuts, vegetable oils, grains, fruit and vegetables don't have any dietary cholesterol.

Cholesterol in food can raise cholesterol in the blood, particularly in people who have a high risk of developing heart disease. However, cholesterol in food does not raise cholesterol in the blood to the same extent as saturated fats. The Heart Foundation recommends that people at high risk of heart disease should restrict their intake of cholesterol-rich foods such as brains, liver, kidneys and other offal foods, and egg yolks.

If your blood cholesterol is okay you can enjoy these foods a little more often.

What about eggs?

The fat and cholesterol in an egg is found in the yolk only. If your doctor says your blood cholesterol level is high, then limit your intake of egg yolks. It is not possible to say how many egg yolks you can eat each week because people's bodies respond differently to cholesterol in food. If you are concerned about this, discuss it with your doctor or Accredited Practising Dietitian.

Should I eat less meat and dairy foods?

Lean red meat, trimmed of visible fat, is low in saturated fat. It is an excellent source of iron, zinc and vitamin B12 and plays an important role in healthy eating. It is very important to limit the amount of full-fat dairy products you eat. Full-fat dairy products are a major source of saturated fat. Low- or reduced-fat dairy products are major sources of calcium in the Australian diet. Calcium plays an important role in preventing the development of osteoporosis (brittle bones).

Which is the best oil to use?

Use a variety of different oils to prepare and cook quick, great-

tastebuds. Fish with the highest amount of healthy fats include atlantic salmon, mackerel, southern blue fin tuna, trevally and sardines. Seafood can also be eaten, as it is low in saturated fat.

Can I use these recipes and health information for my children?

The recipes in this cookbook are suitable for children over two years of age. Offering a variety of foods to children provides a variety of nutrients essential for good health. Variety in colour, texture, flavour, smell and temperature can also spark interest in foods children may not have liked previously. For example, a child may not like a boiled egg alone, but may love scrambled eggs on toast, an omelette with tomato and ham, French toast or a vegetable frittata. Try to offer children new foods – the more children are offered a new food, the more likely they will accept it, especially if they see peers or role models (particularly parents) enjoying the food.

Are very low carbohydrate diets the answer?

Low carbohydrate diets have appeared in the media for many years. The Heart Foundation does not recommend very low carbohydrate diets for long-term weight loss. The Heart Foundation is concerned that the high and unrestricted saturated fat content of many very low carbohydrate diets may increase your risk of heart disease. We are also concerned that many very low carbohydrate diets do not provide adequate nutrition, particularly in dietary folate, calcium and dietary fibre, and that their long-term consequences are not yet known.

What about alcohol?

Alcohol doesn't raise blood cholesterol but it can raise blood triglycerides, blood pressure and body weight. One or two drinks a day may do you no harm, but excessive drinking increases your risk of high blood pressure, heart disease and stroke, as well as many other problems.

For further information about your heart health please call Heartline on 1300 36 27 87 and speak to our trained staff for the cost of a local call or visit Heartsite on www.heartfoundation.com.au

Heart Foundation

tasting meals. Oils such as canola, sunflower, soybean, olive, peanut, macadamia, sesame seed and grapeseed are all suitable. Choose the oil that suits your taste and budget.

What is the best margarine spread to use?

Choose either a polyunsaturated or monounsaturated margarine spread based on sunflower, canola or olive oils.

What about cholesterol-lowering margarine spreads?

The new cholesterol-lowering spreads which have plant sterols added to them have been shown to reduce blood cholesterol levels. To gain the maximum benefit from these, it is recommended that you eat around 1 to $1^1/_2$ tablespoons per day as part of an overall healthy eating pattern.

Am I eating enough fish?

It is a proven fact that eating fish helps to reduce your risk of heart disease. Have fish (any type of fresh or canned) at least twice a week. Choose any fish – whatever is convenient and suits your

Breakfast, Snacks & Lunches

Banana with ricotta and honey on toast

For a delicious savoury version rub the toast, while still hot, with cut cloves of garlic and/or a halved ripe tomato.

Serves **2**
Preparation time **5 minutes**
Cooking time **5 minutes**

100g low-fat ricotta
$1/4$ teaspoon ground cinnamon
2 thick slices sourdough bread (or wholemeal or multigrain)
2 large bananas, peeled and sliced
2 tablespoons chopped raw almonds
2 teaspoons pepitas (pumpkin seeds)
2 teaspoons honey

1. Place the ricotta and ground cinnamon in a bowl and mix well with a fork until smooth. Set aside.
2. Toast the slices of bread under a grill or in a toaster until lightly golden. Spread the slices of toast with an equal quantity of ricotta mixture.
3. Arrange slices of banana on top of the ricotta then sprinkle with almonds and pepitas and drizzle with the honey. Serve immediately.

Nutrients per serve

Energy (kJ)	1470kJ
Energy (cal)	350kcal
Total fat	13.5g
Saturated fat	3.6g
Monounsaturated fat	6.1g
Polyunsaturated fat	2.6g
Protein	13.5g
Carbohydrate	44.8g
Fibre	5.6g
Sodium	285mg
Cholesterol	21.1mg

Porridge with grilled apples, maple syrup and hazelnuts

Serves **2**
Preparation time **5 minutes**
Cooking time **5 minutes**

1 large apple, such as gala or golden delicious
$2/3$ cup quick oats
400ml low-fat milk
2 teaspoons maple syrup
30g hazelnuts, lightly toasted and coarsely chopped

1. Preheat a grill.
2. Core the apple, and then cut across into 1cm slices. Spray lightly with oil. Set a rack about 10cm from the heat source and place the apple slices on foil. Grill until soft and golden, about 5 minutes each side.
3. Meanwhile, combine the oats and milk in a pan and stir until well blended. Bring to a boil and boil for 1 minute. Remove from the heat, stir well and pour into heated serving bowls.
4. Top with the apple slices, drizzle with maple syrup and scatter with hazelnuts. Serve immediately.

The list of fresh fruits to add to porridge is only limited by the seasons and your imagination. Try berries and stonefruits in summer, apples and pears in autumn, citrus fruits in winter and mangoes, pawpaw and passionfruit in springtime. Dried fruits, such as sultanas and apricots are handy stand-bys any time of the year.

Nutrients per serve	
Energy (kJ)	2400kJ
Energy (cal)	573kcal
Total fat	17.2g
Saturated fat	1.9g
Monounsaturated fat	10.5g
Polyunsaturated fat	3.7g
Protein	21.2g
Carbohydrate	83.8g
Fibre	9.7g
Sodium	121mg
Cholesterol	8.0mg

Tomatoes, mushrooms and poached egg on bagel

Serves **4**
Preparation time **10 minutes**
Cooking time **20 minutes**

4 ripe roma tomatoes, halved lengthwise
1 teaspoon canola oil, plus 1 teaspoon extra, for the mushrooms
$1/4$ cup oregano sprigs
250g field mushrooms, thickly sliced
4 very fresh eggs
2 wholegrain bagels, halved and toasted
freshly ground black pepper

1. Preheat the oven to 220°C (200°C fan). Spray an ovenproof dish lightly with oil spray.
2. Arrange the tomatoes, cut sides up, in the prepared dish and drizzle with 1 teaspoon canola oil. Scatter with oregano sprigs and season with pepper. Bake 20 minutes.
3. Meanwhile, heat the extra teaspoon oil in a non-stick frying pan, add the mushrooms and cook until golden, about 5 minutes, turning the slices once.
4. Bring a large pan of water to a boil. Crack the eggs individually into cups or small bowls. When the water is boiling, create a whirlpool by stirring with a wooden spoon. Turn down the heat to simmering, slide in the eggs. Cook until the eggs have just set, but the yolks are still runny, about 3 minutes. Remove with a slotted spoon and drain, on the spoon, on paper towels.
5. Place half a bagel on each plate and top with the mushrooms. Add 2 tomato halves to each and top these with a poached egg. Serve immediately.

In Australia we are now blessed with many good bakeries, making all sorts of interesting breads. Try to eat a wide variety – wholegrain, multigrain, wholemeal, added fibre, and sourdough.

Nutrients per serve	
Energy (kJ)	802kJ
Energy (cal)	192kcal
Total fat	7.0g
Saturated fat	1.7g
Monounsaturated fat	2.9g
Polyunsaturated fat	1.0g
Protein	14.0g
Carbohydrate	17.9g
Fibre	5.1g
Sodium	225mg
Cholesterol	189mg

Prawn salad sandwich

Serves **4**
Preparation time **10 minutes**

500g green prawns
coarsely grated zest of 1 lemon, plus 1 tablespoon freshly squeezed lemon juice
2 teaspoons avocado oil
1 tablespoon chopped fresh dill
4 leaves butter lettuce, rinsed and spun dry
1 cucumber, peeled and thinly sliced
2 wholemeal pita breads
freshly ground black pepper, to taste

1. Bring a large pot of water to a boil,
2. Add the unpeeled prawns and cook 2-3 minutes, until they turn red. Drain and run under cold water. Drain again and dry on paper towels. Peel and devein the prawns and cut them in half lengthwise.
3. Place the prawns in a bowl. Add the lemon zest and juice, oil and dill, and season with pepper.
4. Cut each pita bread in half to serve.
5. Place the lettuce on the bottom half of the opened pitas, Add the cucumber and top this with the prawn salad.

Alternative fillings

1. Mix cooked lean chicken with lemon zest and juice, a little balsamic vinegar and olive oil. Add thinly sliced red onion and serve on sandwiches spread with mustard.
2. Whiz canned drained and rinsed cannellini beans with garlic, lemon juice and a little olive oil. Combine rocket and a few chopped semi-dried tomatoes, stuff into pitas and add bean puree.

**Nutrients per serve
(for prawn salad sandwich)**

Energy (kJ)	1130kJ
Energy (cal)	269kcal
Total fat	3.8g
Saturated fat	0.7g
Monounsaturated fat	1.3g
Polyunsaturated fat	1.0g
Protein	31.6g
Carbohydrate	26.0g
Fibre	4.0g
Sodium	758mg
Cholesterol	235mg

Blue-eye burgers

Serves **6**
Preparation time **15 minutes**
Cooking time **10 minutes**

500g skinless blue-eye fillet
2 cups baby spinach, coarsely chopped, plus 1^1/$_2$ cups extra, for the buns
3 green onions, chopped
1 tablespoon finely chopped fresh ginger
1 egg white
2 teaspoons reduced-salt soy sauce
1 cup fresh breadcrumbs
1 teaspoon peanut oil
6 wholegrain buns
700g oven-roasted thick potato wedges, to serve*
freshly ground black pepper, to taste

1. Cut the blue-eye into pea-sized cubes and combine in a bowl with 2 cups spinach, green onions and ginger, and season with pepper. In another bowl, combine the eggwhite and soy sauce and beat until smooth. Stir into the blue-eye mixture, add the breadcrumbs and, with wet hands, form into six 1cm thick patties.
2. Heat a large, non-stick frying pan over moderate heat and brush with the oil. Cook the burgers 6 minutes on the first side, turn over and cook a further 4 minutes on the other side.
3. Divide the extra 1^1/$_2$ cups spinach among the buns, place a burger on each and serve immediately. Serve with oven-roasted thick potato wedges.

These burgers may also be made with any other firm, white fish, such as blue grenadier, flathead, snapper, bream, or canned tuna.

*To make oven-roasted potato wedges, toss uncooked potato wedges in a large bowl with a little olive oil and toss well to coat. Spread in one layer in a baking dish and bake in a 240°C (220°C fan) oven for 40-60 minutes or until golden and crunchy and cooked through.

Nutrients per serve	
Energy (kJ)	1589kJ
Energy (cal)	382kcal
Total fat	6.2g
Saturated fat	1.6g
Monounsaturated fat	1.8g
Polyunsaturated fat	1.9g
Protein	29.2g
Carbohydrate	50.8g
Fibre	6.1g
Sodium	670mg
Cholesterol	58.3mg

Smoked salmon pizza

Serves **6**
Preparation time **5 minutes**
Cooking time **15 minutes**

   200g low-fat ricotta
   $1/4$ cup low-fat plain yoghurt
   1 prepared wholemeal pizza base
   1 punnet cherry tomatoes, halved
   $1/4$ cup snipped chives
   100g smoked salmon, cut into strips
   10g baby rocket leaves (about 30 leaves)
   1 tablespoon green peppercorns, drained

1. Preheat the oven to 230°C (210°C fan).
2. Combine the ricotta and yoghurt in a bowl and whisk with a fork until smooth. Spread on the prepared pizza base and scatter with the tomatoes and chives. Bake 15 minutes, or until the crust is crisp and golden. Remove from the oven and cool on a wire rack for 5 minutes.
3. Drape the salmon over the pizza and top with the baby rocket. Sprinkle with the green peppercorns. Serve immediately.

The sky's the limit when it comes to healthy pizza toppings. Try roast potato or pumpkin, capsicum, mushrooms, shallots, lean ham or barbecued chicken without skin.

Nutrients per serve	
Energy (kJ)	1300kJ
Energy (cal)	311kcal
Total fat	6.9g
Saturated fat	2.4g
Monounsaturated fat	1.8g
Polyunsaturated fat	1.4g
Protein	15.6g
Carbohydrate	46.0g
Fibre	3.9g
Sodium	824mg
Cholesterol	23.1mg

Sweet potato pancakes with papaya salsa

Serves **6**
Preparation time **20 minutes**
Cooking time **20 minutes**

2 eggwhites
1 tablespoon curry powder
$1/4$ teaspoon tabasco
$1^1/2$ tablespoons freshly squeezed lemon juice
$1/2$ cup plain flour
1 red onion, coarsely grated
500g sweet potato, coarsely grated
canola oil cooking spray

PAPAYA SALSA
600g papaya, cut into 1cm cubes
1 roma tomato, seeded and cut into $1/2$ cm cubes
1 tablespoon freshly squeezed lemon juice
1 hot red chilli, thinly sliced (optional)
2 tablespoons coarsely chopped coriander leaves
freshly ground black pepper, to taste

1. Preheat the oven to 230°C (210°C fan).
2. To make the papaya salsa, combine the papaya, tomato, lemon juice, chilli, if used and coriander in a bowl and mix gently. Set aside.
3. Lightly beat the eggwhites in a bowl, stir in the curry powder, tabasco, pepper and lemon juice. Whisk in the flour.
4. Combine the onion and sweet potato in a bowl and mix well. Squeeze to remove excess liquid. Combine with the eggwhite mixture.
5. Place 2 baking sheets in the oven for 5 minutes. Line with baking paper and spray the paper lightly with oil. With a large spoon, dollop the mixture onto the baking sheets and flatten. Spray lightly with oil and bake 8 minutes. Turn over, spray lightly with oil again and cook a further 8 minutes, or until the pancakes are tender. Serve immediately, with the salsa.

Papaya is available in spring. Other times of the year this salsa is equally good when made with pawpaw, mango, rockmelon, peach or nectarines.

Nutrients per serve	
Energy (kJ)	593kJ
Energy (cal)	142kcal
Total fat	0.5g
Saturated fat	0.0g
Monounsaturated fat	0.1g
Polyunsaturated fat	0.1g
Protein	5.2g
Carbohydrate	28.7g
Fibre	5.3g
Sodium	44mg
Cholesterol	0.0mg

Asparagus, pea and parsley rice

Serves **4**
Preparation time **10 minutes**
Cooking time **30 minutes**

1 tablespoon extra virgin olive oil
1 large onion, chopped
2 cloves garlic, finely chopped
1^1/$_2$ cups (300g) basmati rice
4 cups (1 litre) reduced-salt chicken stock
1 bunch thin green asparagus, woody bottoms snapped off, spears diagonally cut into
  4cm pieces
250g peas in the pod, shelled, or 1 cup frozen peas
^{1}/$_4$ cup grated parmesan cheese
2 tablespoons chopped flat-leaf parsley
freshly ground black pepper, to taste

1. Combine the oil and onion in a pan with a well-fitting lid and cook over moderate heat until onion is soft, about 5 minutes, stirring frequently. Add the garlic and stir a further 1 minute.
2. Stir in the rice and stock and season with pepper. Bring to a simmer, cover with a lid, then turn heat down to low and simmer for 14 minutes. Place the asparagus and peas on top of the rice, replace the lid and simmer a further 6 minutes.
3. Stir in the parmesan and parsley and serve immediately in deep, heated plates.

Although fresh is always best, excellent results can be obtained with frozen varieties, such as peas, corn, beans and mixed vegetables, without any significant loss of flavour and nutrients.

Nutrients per serve	
Energy (kJ)	1632kJ
Energy (cal)	396kcal
Total fat	8.5g
Saturated fat	2.5g
Monounsaturated fat	4.6g
Polyunsaturated fat	0.7g
Protein	12.5g
Carbohydrate	65.2g
Fibre	6.1g
Sodium	795mg
Cholesterol	7.6mg

Vegetarian lasagne

Serves **6**
Preparation time **20 minutes**
Cooking time **40 minutes**

1 tablespoon extra virgin olive oil
1 large leek, white part only, well rinsed and thinly sliced
1 bunch rocket, tough stems removed, leaves well rinsed and spun dry, coarsely chopped
75g (^{1}/$_3$ cup) low-fat ricotta cheese
75g (^{1}/$_3$ cup) low-fat cottage cheese
400g eggplant, cut in 5mm thick slices
2 green zucchini, trimmed and sliced lengthwise in 5mm thick slices
1 large red capsicum, halved, seeds removed and cut into 4cm pieces
300g jap pumpkin, skin and seeds removed and cut into 5mm thick slices
3 sheets ready to cook lasagne, approx 18cm x 25cm
2 cups (500ml) reduced-salt tomato pasta sauce
^{1}/$_4$ cup freshly grated parmesan cheese
freshly ground black pepper, to taste

1. Preheat the oven to 190°C (170°C fan).
2. Combine the oil and leek in a large, non-stick frying pan and season with pepper. Cook over moderate heat until the leek is golden brown, about 15 minutes, stirring from time to time. Add the rocket and cook a further 1-2 minutes, or until wilted. Stir in the cheeses and set aside.
3. Meanwhile heat a grill or barbecue until very hot. Place the eggplant on the grill and cook for approximately 3 minutes on each side, then set aside. Lightly spray the zucchini slices with olive oil spray then place on the grill and cook for 2 minutes on each side, then set aside. Lightly spray the capsicum and pumpkin with olive oil spray and cook for 3-5 minutes on each side then remove from the grill and place with the other vegetables
4. Bring a large pot of water to a boil. Cook the lasagne for 2 minutes, drain and set aside on clean tea towels.
5. Smear the bottom of a baking dish with a few tablespoons of the tomato sauce then place one sheet of the pasta on the bottom. Top the pasta with half of the grilled vegetables and pour over a third of the tomato sauce. Spoon over half of the leek and cheese mixture then place another sheet of pasta on top and create a second layer with the remaining ingredients. Place the third pasta sheet on the lasagna to create the third layer and spoon over the remaining tomato sauce and sprinkle with the grated parmesan cheese.
6. Cover the dish with foil and bake for 30 minutes. Remove the foil and cook a further 10 minutes or until the top is golden and the sauce is bubbling.

The current Dietary Guidelines for Australia recommend adults eat at least 4 serves of cereals (including breads, rice, pasta or noodles) each day, preferably wholegrain.

Nutrients per serve	
Energy (kJ)	882kJ
Energy (cal)	212kcal
Total fat	7.2g
Saturated fat	2.4g
Monounsaturated fat	3.4g
Polyunsaturated fat	0.8g
Protein	10.6g
Carbohydrate	26.0g
Fibre	5.4g
Sodium	400mg
Cholesterol	10.8mg

Pasta with fresh pea pesto

Serves **6**
Preparation time **20 minutes**
Cooking time **15 minutes**

250g shelled peas (about 900g before shelling) or 1 cup frozen peas
2 large cloves garlic, finely chopped
30g pinenuts or blanched almonds, lightly toasted
30g chopped parmesan cheese
$^1/_2$ cup fresh mint leaves
375g dry pasta, such as linguine
1 tablespoon extra virgin olive oil
freshly ground black pepper, to taste

1. Plunge the peas into boiling water and cook 2-3 minutes, or until just tender, but still crisp. Drain and refresh under cold water. Pat dry.
2. To make the pesto, combine the peas, garlic, pinenuts, cheese, mint and olive oil in a processor and pulse until coarsely chopped. Season with pepper and transfer to a large pasta bowl.
3. Meanwhile, cook the pasta in boiling water until al dente. Drain, reserving a cup of the cooking water. Add enough of the cooking water to the pesto to moisten. Add the pasta and toss well, adding more of the cooking water, if necessary. Serve immediately in heated bowls.

Why not try this fabulous recipe using broadbeans instead of the peas. It will look the same, but it will taste different.

Nutrients per serve	
Energy (kJ)	752kJ
Energy (cal)	180kcal
Total fat	7.9g
Saturated fat	1.7g
Monounsaturated fat	4.5g
Polyunsaturated fat	1.1g
Protein	7.8g
Carbohydrate	19.3g
Fibre	5.3g
Sodium	112mg
Cholesterol	4.7mg

Soups & Starters

Classic minestrone

Minestrone in Italy is made using "cavolo nero" (black cabbage), a crinkly dark green cabbage which needs to grow in a cold climate. As this cabbage isn't readily available in Australia, the next best thing for authentic flavour is savoy cabbage.
You could also use Chinese, napa, or white or red cabbage.

Serves **6**
Preparation time **30 minutes**
Cooking time **3 hours, 20 minutes**

125g dried cannellini beans, or a 400g can cannellini beans, well rinsed
30g pancetta, trimmed of fat, finely chopped
$^1/_3$ cup flat-leaf parsley
2 cloves garlic, peeled
2 teaspoons extra virgin olive oil
2 large onions, sliced
4 carrots, halved lengthwise, cut into 1cm pieces
2 stalks celery, sliced
$^1/_2$ cauliflower, cut into 2cm flowerets
2 medium desiree potatoes, peeled and cubed
2 zucchini, sliced
125g green beans, cut into 2cm pieces
1 cup frozen peas
250g savoy cabbage, thinly sliced
400g can reduced-salt diced roma tomatoes, with juice
2 tablespoons parmesan cheese shavings

1. Place the cannellini beans in a saucepan with plenty of water to cover, bring to a boil, boil for 2 minutes, remove from the heat and leave to soak for 1 hour. Drain and rinse well. Return to the saucepan with about 2.5cm water to cover and bring slowly to a boil. Simmer until the beans are tender, about 30-60 minutes, depending on age. Reserve in the cooking liquid and set aside.
2. Combine the pancetta, parsley and garlic in a processor and pulse until finely chopped and then transfer to a large, heavy-based saucepan with the oil. Place over medium-low heat and saute for 2 minutes. Add onion and cook until onion is soft, about 5 minutes, stirring frequently. Add carrots and stir over heat for a few minutes, before adding the celery, cauliflower, potatoes, zucchini, green beans, peas and cabbage, each one in turn, stirring each for a few minutes before adding the next. Cook until the cabbage has wilted, stirring occasionally.
3. Add enough water to just cover the vegetables. Add the tomatoes with their juice. Cover the pot and cook at a gentle simmer, just the occasional bubble on the surface, for 2 hours.
4. When ready to serve, add the reserved cannellini beans and heat through for 10 minutes. Remove from the heat and scatter parmesan shavings on top. Serve hot or warm.

Nutrients per serve

Energy (kJ)	1230kJ
Energy (cal)	294kcal
Total fat	5.2g
Saturated fat	1.1g
Monounsaturated fat	2.3g
Polyunsaturated fat	0.5g
Protein	20.8g
Carbohydrate	41.6g
Fibre	20.0g
Sodium	283mg
Cholesterol	5.8mg

Chicken soup with green beans, broad beans and rice

Serves **6**
Preparation time **10 minutes**
Cooking time **25 minutes**

1 tablespoon extra virgin olive oil
1 small red onion, chopped
2 large cloves garlic, finely chopped
350g chicken breast
125g stringless green beans, cut into 2cm pieces
5 cups (1.25 litres) salt-reduced chicken stock
125g long grain white rice
100g fresh or frozen broadbeans, tough skins removed
1/4 cup shredded fresh basil
freshly ground black pepper

1. Combine the oil and onion in a pan and cook over moderate heat until soft, about 5 minutes. Add the garlic and cook a further 1 minute. Increase the heat and add the chicken and cook for 3-5 minutes or until golden brown and tender. Remove the chicken from the pan and set aside. Reduce the heat and add the green beans and chicken stock and bring to a boil.
2. Add rice and simmer 10 minutes, stirring from time to time. Add broadbeans and simmer until beans and rice are tender, about 6-8 minutes, adding more boiling water if soup becomes too thick. Add the reserved chicken tenderloins then stir in the basil and season with pepper. Serve immediately in heated plates or bowls.

A very low-salt stock is easily made at home. If you use prepared stock, make sure it's reduced-salt stock. To reduce the salt content even further, substitute part of the stock volume with water or wine. You can add flavour with herbs and spices, such as garlic, onion, lemon, chilli or mint.

Nutrients per serve

Energy (kJ)	1130kJ
Energy (cal)	270kcal
Total fat	6.6g
Saturated fat	1.5g
Monounsaturated fat	3.6g
Polyunsaturated fat	0.8g
Protein	17.2g
Carbohydrate	35.0g
Fibre	2.0g
Sodium	725mg
Cholesterol	38.5mg

Tomato and butter bean soup with toast

Serves **4**
Preparation time **15 minutes**
Cooking time **20 minutes**

1 tablespoon extra virgin olive oil
1 red onion, peeled and finely chopped
2 cloves garlic, peeled and finely chopped
$1/2$ teaspoon chilli powder (optional)
2 x 400g tins reduced-salt chopped tomatoes
1 teaspoon sugar
freshly ground black pepper
2 cups salt-reduced chicken or vegetable stock
1 x 400g can butter beans, drained and well rinsed
$1/4$ cup basil leaves
2 tablespoons parmesan shavings

TOAST
2 small multigrain rolls cut into 8 slices
olive oil spray

1. Heat the oil in a large saucepan over a medium heat then add the onion and cook for 5 minutes or until soft. Add the garlic and chilli powder if using, and cook for a further minute.
2. Pour in the canned tomatoes and add the sugar and black pepper and cook for 5 minutes uncovered.
3. Add the chicken stock and bring the soup to the boil then reduce the heat and allow to simmer for 15 minutes uncovered.
4. To make the toast heat a barbecue or grill pan until very hot. Lightly spray the bread slices with olive oil spray and place on the grill and grill for 2-3 minutes on each side or until golden and grill marks are visable. Place the toast on a plate and cover with foil to keep warm.
5. Add the butter beans to the soup and cook for 3 minutes to heat through, then stir in the basil leaves and serve in bowls. Top with shaved parmesan and serve with the toast.

Where possible, use "reduced-salt" or "no added salt" ingredients such as canned vegetables, sauces and stock. Use the Heart Foundation Tick as your guide in the supermarket to make healthier choices. Tick products are lower in saturated fat and salt, and some contain limited kilojoules and are higher in dietary fibre.

Nutrients per serve

Energy (kJ)	824kJ
Energy (cal)	197kcal
Total fat	7.2g
Saturated fat	1.5g
Monounsaturated fat	3.8g
Polyunsaturated fat	1.1g
Protein	8.4g
Carbohydrate	24.4g
Fibre	6.9g
Sodium	728mg
Cholesterol	3.1mg

Prawn and mango spring rolls

Serves **4**
Preparation time **30 minutes**

8 green king prawns, peeled
90g vermicelli rice noodles
2 tablespoons rice vinegar
1 tablespoon sugar
8 x 20cm rice paper spring roll wrappers
$^1/_2$ cup coriander, leaves only
$^1/_2$ cup mint, leaves only
$^1/_2$ seedless cucumber, peeled, seeds removed, cut into matchsticks
2 green onions, cut into matchsticks
250g ripe, but firm mango, cut into $^1/_2$cm sticks

DIPPING SAUCE
1 tablespoon fish sauce
1 tablespoon freshly squeezed lime juice
1 tablespoon water
1 teaspoon palm sugar or brown sugar

1. To make the dipping sauce, combine the fish sauce, lime juice, water and sugar in a small bowl and stir until the sugar has dissolved. Set aside.
2. Bring a large pot of water to a boil, add the prawns. When they turn opaque, remove them with a slotted spoon and cool under cold running water. Dry on paper towels and cut in half lengthwise. Set aside.
3. Add the rice noodles to the boiling water and cook until tender, about 2 minutes. Drain in a colander, run under cold water, drain again and place in a bowl. Combine the rice vinegar and sugar in a small bowl, pour over the noodles and toss to coat.
4. Soak the rice papers, one at a time, in warm water for 30 seconds, then place on a wet surface. Arrange a couple of coriander leaves in the middle of the round, place two of the prawn halves, cut side down, on top of the coriander and spread with $^1/_4$ cup of the noodles. Then arrange about 3 mint leaves, 8 cucumber sticks, 6 green onion sticks and a few mango sticks horizontally over the noodles. Roll the rice paper, folding in ends, stopping about halfway to add 3 more coriander and mint leaves. Place the rolls seam down on a plate and cover with a clean, damp tea towel. Serve the rolls whole or halved diagonally, with the dipping sauce.

Prawns are low in saturated fat, although they do contain dietary cholesterol. Eating prawns once a week or less is unlikely to affect your cholesterol levels. Rice paper wrappers (bahn tran in Vietnamese) are available in Oriental stores or supermarkets – don't confuse them with the edible "rice" paper which is used for sweet confections, such as nougat or macaroons.

Nutrients per serve	
Energy (kJ)	880kJ
Energy (cal)	210kcal
Total fat	0.6g
Saturated fat	0.1g
Monounsaturated fat	0.1g
Polyunsaturated fat	0.1g
Protein	16.6g
Carbohydrate	33.1g
Fibre	1.3g
Sodium	704mg
Cholesterol	111.8mg

Lemon risotto with rocket

Serves **4**
Preparation time **10 minutes**
Cooking time **30 minutes**

3 cups (750ml) reduced-salt chicken stock
3 cups (750ml) water
2 teaspoons extra virgin olive oil
1 onion, chopped
2 teaspoons coarsely grated lemon zest, plus 2 tablespoons freshly squeezed lemon juice
2 large cloves garlic, finely chopped
400g arborio rice
$^1/_2$ cup (125ml) dry white wine
30g freshly grated parmesan cheese
200g rocket, well rinsed, spun dry and cut into strips
freshly ground black pepper, to taste

1. Combine the chicken stock and water in a pan and bring to a simmer.
2. Combine the oil and onion in a heavy, round-bottomed saucepan and cook over moderate heat until the onion is soft, about 5 minutes, stirring frequently. Add the lemon zest and garlic, and stir a further 1 minute.
3. Add the rice and stir 2 minutes to coat the grains. Add the wine and stir until absorbed. Add a ladleful of the simmering stock and stir until absorbed. Continue adding stock in this manner until the rice is tender, about 20 minutes. Reserve a few tablespoons of the stock to stir in last. Season with pepper halfway through the cooking time. If the stock runs out before the rice is cooked, continue with simmering water.
4. When the rice is cooked, add the reserved stock and the reserved lemon juice, the parmesan and rocket, and stir vigorously. Cover the pan and stand 3 minutes before serving in warmed, deep plates.

Although there are many different imported Italian rices which are ideal to make risotto, the most common variety is arborio, which is now grown in Australia. Other specific risotto rices available in Australia are vialone nano, for a very creamy and smooth result, or carnaroli, which won't easily overcook and never becomes mushy.

Nutrients per serve	
Energy (kJ)	1892kJ
Energy (cal)	459kcal
Total fat	6.0g
Saturated fat	2.2g
Monounsaturated fat	2.8g
Polyunsaturated fat	0.5g
Protein	11.6g
Carbohydrate	81.6g
Fibre	4.2g
Sodium	641mg
Cholesterol	7.4mg

Pasta with grilled asparagus, lemon and basil

Serves **4**
Preparation time **10 minutes**
Cooking time **15 minutes**

500g thin asparagus spears, woody ends broken off
1 teaspoon extra virgin olive oil, plus 3 teaspoons extra
freshly squeezed juice of 1 lemon, plus wedges, to serve
400g dry pasta (either long, such as linguine, or short, such as casareccia or penne)
4 large cloves garlic, finely sliced
2 hot red chillies, thinly sliced
1/2 cup fresh basil leaves
30g (1/2 cup) freshly grated parmesan cheese
freshly ground black pepper

1. Preheat a stovetop griller or an overhead griller.
2. Spray the asparagus with a little olive oil spray and grill them until tender and slightly charred. Remove from the griller and cut into bite-sized pieces. Toss in a bowl with the oil and half the lemon juice, and season with pepper. Set aside.
3. Cook the pasta in boiling water until al dente and drain, reserving a small jugful of the cooking water.

4. Meanwhile, combine the remaining oil with the garlic and chillies in a large, non-stick frying pan and cook over low heat until garlic is fragrant, about 5 minutes. Add about 1/3 cup of the cooking water and the remaining lemon juice and bring to a boil. Add the reserved asparagus and the drained pasta and toss over heat, adding more of the cooking water to moisten.
5. Transfer to a heated bowl, add the basil and parmesan and toss again, adding more cooking water to moisten as necessary. Serve immediately, with lemon wedges separately.

Grilling asparagus (and many other vegetables) really intensifies their flavour. The secret about grilling them without scorching and sticking is to coat them very lightly with oil before putting them on the grill. Remember to always heat the grill well, but don't oil it – only the food that's being cooked.

Nutrients per serve	
Energy (kJ)	1730kJ
Energy (cal)	413kcal
Total fat	6.0g
Saturated fat	2.1g
Monounsaturated fat	2.4g
Polyunsaturated fat	0.8g
Protein	17.5g
Carbohydrate	70.8g
Fibre	5.8g
Sodium	129mg
Cholesterol	7.1mg

Pasta with tomato, chilli and borlotti beans

Serves **4**
Preparation time **5 minutes**
Cooking time **30 minutes**

400g long pasta, such as fettuccine
1 green chilli, thinly sliced, seeds removed, if you like
400g can borlotti beans, drained and well rinsed
freshly squeezed juice of $1/2$ lemon

TOMATO SAUCE
1 tablespoon olive oil
1 onion, peeled and chopped
1 large clove garlic, finely chopped
2 x 400g can Italian diced tomatoes, with juice (preferably reduced-salt)
freshly ground black pepper, to taste

1. Make the tomato sauce first: combine the oil and onion in a pan and cook over moderate heat until soft, about 5 minutes, stirring frequently. Add the garlic and cook a further 1-2 minutes, then stir in the tomatoes with their juice and bring to a boil. Simmer for 10 minutes or until the sauce thickens and season with pepper.
2. Cook the pasta in plenty of boiling water until al dente.
3. Meanwhile, add the chilli and drained beans to the tomato sauce and heat through, stirring from time to time. Stir in the lemon juice.
4. Drain the pasta, reserving a cup of the cooking water. Add the pasta to the tomato sauce, together with half a cup of the reserved cooking water. Stir over brisk heat for 2 minutes. Serve the pasta in deep, heated plates.

Fresh borlotti beans are available intermittently during the year. When you see them in their beautiful pink and cream pods, buy a kilo and you'll be richly rewarded. To cook, remove them from their pods (you'll end up with about 400g beans) and cook them in simmering unsalted water, with perhaps a few sage leaves and a few bruised garlic cloves. Simmer until tender, about 30 minutes.

Nutrients per serve

Energy (kJ)	2270kJ
Energy (cal)	542kcal
Total fat	4.4g
Saturated fat	0.7g
Monounsaturated fat	1.7g
Polyunsaturated fat	0.9g
Protein	22.4g
Carbohydrate	104g
Fibre	10.5g
Sodium	146mg
Cholesterol	0.0mg

Mains

Cumin pork on couscous

Couscous consists of little balls of wheat-based dough, and is often mistaken for a grain. You can find a wide variety in your supermarket, some of them flavoured with tomatoes, onions and other flavourings. The plain variety is a delicious alternative to rice or pasta, and is quick and easy to prepare.

Serves **4**
Preparation time **20 minutes**
Cooking time **15 minutes**

480g pork fillets, cut into 4 equal pieces
1 tablespoon sunflower oil
2 teaspoons ground cumin
freshly ground black pepper, to taste
freshly squeezed juice of $1/2$ lemon
500g steamed zucchini, sliced, to serve

COUSCOUS
300g instant couscous
1 clove garlic, finely chopped
$1/3$ cup freshly squeezed lemon juice
2 teaspoons ground cumin
$1/2$ bunch green onions, both white and green parts, finely sliced
$1/2$ cup coarsely chopped flat-leaf parsley
ground black pepper, to taste

1. Preheat the oven to 180°C (160°C fan).
2. Brush the pork with the oil, then rub all over with cumin and pepper. Place in a dish, add the lemon juice and turn several times to coat well. Set aside.
3. Combine the couscous in a bowl with $1^1/2$ cups (375ml) boiling water, stand 5 minutes or until water has been absorbed. Fluff with a fork and stir in the garlic, lemon juice, cumin, green onion and parsley. Season with pepper and set aside.
4. Heat a heavy-based non-stick frying pan, add the pork and brown on all sides. Transfer the pan to the oven and bake 5-8 minutes. Remove from the oven, place the pork on a plate and tent loosely with foil. Stand 5 minutes, then slice and serve with the couscous and the steamed zucchini.

Nutrients per serve	
Energy (kJ)	2000kJ
Energy (cal)	477kcal
Total fat	8.2g
Saturated fat	1.5g
Monounsaturated fat	2.3g
Polyunsaturated fat	3.3g
Protein	38.0g
Carbohydrate	60.9g
Fibre	3.4g
Sodium	104mg
Cholesterol	113mg

Steamed salmon with salsa verde

Serves **4**
Preparation time **15 minutes**
Cooking time **10 minutes**

4 skinless salmon fillets, 150g each
500g steamed green beans, to serve

SALSA VERDE
1 cup flat-leaf parsley leaves
1 cup fresh coriander leaves
$1/2$ stalk celery, chopped
4 cloves garlic, peeled
1 teaspoons drained capers
2 tablespoons freshly squeezed lemon juice
2 tablespoons water

1. To make the salsa verde, combine the parsley, coriander, celery, garlic, capers, lemon juice and water in a processor and whiz until the mixture is roughly chopped. Set aside.
2. Place the salmon fillets on a plate. Place in a steamer basket in a wok containing enough water to create steam. Bring to a boil. Spoon half the salsa verde over the salmon.
Cover the wok and steam for 7 minutes or until the fish flakes easily. Alternatively, if you don't have a steamer basket or a wok, place another plate upside down in a large pan, creating a platform. Add enough water to create steam. Place the plate containing the salmon on top, spoon half of the salsa verde over the salmon, cover pan with a lid and bring water to a boil. Steam salmon as above.
3. Transfer the salmon and beans to heated plates. Stir any liquid remaining on the steaming plate into the remaining salsa verde and pour over the salmon and beans. Serve immediately.

Salsa verde literally means green sauce and is a classic stand-by in the Italian kitchen to accompany plain roasted fish, poultry or meats. Another fresh sauce to try: combine 500g chopped ripe tomatoes with $1/4$ cup chopped brown shallots, 2 tablespoons red wine vinegar, handfuls of torn basil and coarsely chopped parsley, and season with plenty of freshly ground black pepper.

Nutrients per serve	
Energy (kJ)	1050kJ
Energy (cal)	251kcal
Total fat	11.1g
Saturated fat	2.4g
Monounsaturated fat	3.0g
Polyunsaturated fat	4.1g
Protein	33.2g
Carbohydrate	4.0g
Fibre	6.1g
Sodium	109mg
Cholesterol	78.0mg

Thin beefsteaks with watercress, tomato, olives and basil

Serves **4**
Preparation time **15 minutes**
Cooking time **5 minutes**

- 8 small beef fillet steaks, about 60g each, trimmed and pounded to $^1/_2$cm thickness
- 1 tablespoon safflower oil
- 4 roma tomatoes, cut into cubes
- $^1/_3$ cup kalamata olives, stoned and roughly chopped
- 40g basil, tough stems removed, leaves roughly torn
- 4 cups watercress sprigs, tough stems removed
- freshly ground black pepper

1. Place the beef on a large plate and brush with oil. Turn the steaks once, to coat them well, and set aside.
2. Combine the tomatoes, olives and basil in a bowl and season with pepper. Toss well and set aside to amalgamate flavours. Line a large platter with the watercress.
3. Cook the beef, without crowding, on a very hot stovetop griller or in a heated, non-stick frying pan, until just seared on the outside, about 30 seconds each side. Remove each steak and set aside to rest for 5 minutes. Season the meat with pepper.
4. Arrange steaks on the watercress and spoon the tomato mixture over. Serve immediately, with extra oil for drizzling.

Watercress is at its peak from November to March, but any other time of the year try baby rocket as an alternative. Always make sure you rinse watercress in a large basin until no more grit remains.

Nutrients per serve	
Energy (kJ)	991kJ
Energy (cal)	237kcal
Total fat	11.0g
Saturated fat	3.0g
Monounsaturated fat	3.4g
Polyunsaturated fat	3.7g
Protein	28.1g
Carbohydrate	5.7g
Fibre	4.2g
Sodium	201mg
Cholesterol	80.3mg

Thai chicken stir-fry

Serves **6**
Preparation time **15 minutes**
Cooking time **6 minutes**

1 tablespoon peanut oil
3 cloves garlic, finely chopped
450g skinless, boneless chicken breasts, cut into 1cm strips
2 hot red chillies, sliced
2 teaspoons fish sauce
2 teaspoons caster sugar
$^1/_4$ teaspoon freshly ground black pepper
2 tablespoons water
$^3/_4$ cup fresh coriander leaves
$^3/_4$ cup fresh basil leaves
500g (4 small bunches) bok choy, leaves separated
2 tablespoons freshly squeezed lime juice, plus lime wedges, to serve
steamed rice, to serve

1. Heat a wok or large frying pan over high heat, add oil and when hot, but not smoking, add garlic and stir-fry until the garlic starts to colour, about 30 seconds.
2. Add chicken and stir-fry until white, about 3 minutes. Add chillies, fish sauce, sugar, pepper and water, and stir-fry 1 minute.
3. Add coriander, basil and bok choy and stir-fry a further 1 minute. Stir in lime juice and serve with rice and lime wedges.

Stir-frying has become one of the most popular forms of cooking in Australia, judging by the number of households claiming to own one or more woks. Almost any vegetable can be stir-fried. Try cauliflower, snow peas, broccoli, asparagus and mushrooms. Make sure the vegetables are cut into sizes that will allow them to cook at the same time, or stagger the times when they enter the wok.

Nutrients per serve	
Energy (kJ)	1860kJ
Energy (cal)	446kcal
Total fat	7.8g
Saturated fat	1.9g
Monounsaturated fat	3.1g
Polyunsaturated fat	1.7g
Protein	23.0g
Carbohydrate	69.9g
Fibre	2.6g
Sodium	186mg
Cholesterol	49.3mg

Chicken curry with coriander and tomato

Serves **6**
Preparation time **20 minutes, plus overnight standing**
Cooking time **20 minutes**

700g skinless, boneless chicken breast, cut into large bite-sized pieces
2 large green capsicum, seeds and membranes removed, thinly sliced
2 cups fresh coriander, tough stems removed, leaves coarsely chopped
2 large cloves garlic, finely chopped
5cm piece fresh ginger, thinly sliced
freshly squeezed juice of 2 lemons
1 tablespoon red curry paste
1 tablespoon peanut oil
6 roma tomatoes, chopped, with skin on

1. Combine the chicken, capsicum, coriander, garlic, ginger, lemon juice and red curry in a large bowl and toss well to coat. Refrigerate overnight, if possible, turning from time to time.
2. Heat the oil in a large pan over moderate heat, add the chicken and capsicum and all of the marinade, and saute until the chicken is nearly cooked, about 10 minutes.
3. Add the tomatoes and cook a further 5-10 minutes, or until the chicken is cooked through and the tomatoes are hot. Serve hot.

We tend to think of a curry as a dish that takes forever to cook, or otherwise something that comes out of a jar. This delicious curry cooks in only 20 minutes and it's literally bursting with fresh fragrance. What's more, it freezes like a dream, so why not cook up a big batch for several rainy days.

Nutrients per serve	
Energy (kJ)	1630kJ
Energy (cal)	389kcal
Total fat	8.6g
Saturated fat	2.3g
Monounsaturated fat	3.4g
Polyunsaturated fat	1.5g
Protein	31.5g
Carbohydrate	45.0g
Fibre	4.4g
Sodium	94mg
Cholesterol	76.9mg

Spiced lime lamb cutlets

Serves **4**
Preparation time **10 minutes**, plus 15 minutes standing
Cooking time **6 minutes**

3 large cloves garlic, finely chopped
$1/2$ teaspoon ground cardamom
$1/4$ teaspoon ground cumin
$1/4$ cup freshly squeezed lime juice
$1/2$ teaspoon coarsely ground black pepper
2 teaspoons sunflower oil, plus 2 teaspoons extra
8 lean lamb cutlets (450g), about 1cm thick, any visible fat removed
500g steamed cauliflowerets
4 cups boiled rice seasoned with 2 tablespoons finely chopped onion, 2 tablespoons
    freshly squeezed lemon juice and freshly ground black pepper, to serve

1. Combine the garlic, cardamom, cumin, lime juice, pepper and 2 teaspoons of oil in
a large dish, add lamb cutlets and marinate at room temperature for 15 minutes, turning
them once or twice.
2. Heat a large, non-stick frying pan over high heat, add the extra oil and as soon as the oil is
hot, but not smoking, add the lamb in 1 layer. Cook 3 minutes each side for medium rare.
Transfer lamb to a platter, cover loosely with foil and stand 5 minutes before serving. If your
pan is not large enough to hold the cutlets comfortably in one layer, cook the lamb in batches.
3. While the lamb is resting, add the steamed cauliflowerets with $1/3$ cup water to
the pan and saute in the spicy residue to heat through. Serve cauliflower with the lamb
and the seasoned rice.

Serve these fabulous lamb cutlets with a large salad or serve a variety of vegetables (a good idea for every main meal). Look at our salad and vegetable recipes for further inspiration.

Nutrients per serve	
Energy (kJ)	2070kJ
Energy (cal)	494kcal
Total fat	15.0g
Saturated fat	5.2g
Monounsaturated fat	5.2g
Polyunsaturated fat	2.9g
Protein	31.4g
Carbohydrate	56.8g
Fibre	3.8g
Sodium	366mg
Cholesterol	76.4mg

Baked meatballs with mozzarella

Serves **6**
Preparation time **20 minutes**
Cooking time **40 minutes**

2 slices Italian-type bread, crusts removed, soaked in low-fat milk
500g minced lean beef
1 large clove garlic, finely chopped
15g freshly grated parmesan, plus 15g extra, for the top
1 teaspoon grated lemon zest
1 tablespoon chopped fresh oregano leaves
2 large eggs
1 tablespoon extra virgin olive oil
400g can reduced-salt diced roma tomatoes, with juice
2 cups fresh basil leaves, roughly torn
50g shredded reduced fat mozzarella
500g steamed savoy cabbage wedges, to serve
freshly ground black pepper
6 cups cooked risoni (rice-shaped pasta), to serve

1. Preheat the oven to 200°C (180°C fan) and spray an 8-cup ovenproof dish with olive oil spray.
2. Squeeze the bread to remove milk and combine in a bowl with the mince, garlic, 15g parmesan, lemon zest, oregano and the eggs. Season with pepper, make a little patty and fry to check seasoning.
3. Shape the mixture into balls and refrigerate to firm up, if time permits. Heat a heavy-based frying pan or casserole over moderately high heat, add the oil and when hot but not smoking, add the balls. Cook until golden brown on all sides, shaking the pan frequently.
4. Add the tomatoes and cook until the sauce slightly thickens. Stir in half the basil. Transfer the mixture to the prepared dish and cover with the mozzarella. Tuck in the basil here and there and scatter with the extra parmesan. Bake 20 minutes, or until the cheese is golden and the filling is bubbling.
5. Serve with steamed savoy cabbage wedges and risoni.

Choose lean mince as it is lower in saturated fat. It is available from most supermarkets and butchers. Premium lean mince is more expensive than regular mince, however it contains very little fat and therefore doesn't shrink as much during cooking.

Nutrients per serve	
Energy (kJ)	1800kJ
Energy (cal)	431kcal
Total fat	13.9g
Saturated fat	4.9g
Monounsaturated fat	6.1g
Polyunsaturated fat	1.2g
Protein	31.7g
Carbohydrate	44.3g
Fibre	7.1g
Sodium	311mg
Cholesterol	125mg

Roast beef with thyme and port sauce

Serves **6**
Preparation time **10 minutes**
Cooking time **45-60 minutes, plus 20 minutes standing**

720g lean beef, such as fillet or sirloin, any visible fat removed
1 tablespoon extra virgin olive oil
1 large red onion, coarsely chopped
1 large bunch thyme
$1/4$ cup (60ml) port

MASHED POTATOES
1 kg desiree potatoes, peeled and cut in 4cm chunks
$1/2$ cup low-fat milk, warmed
freshly ground black pepper

600g steamed vegetables of your choice, to serve (try asparagus and yellow squash)
freshly ground black pepper, to taste

1. Preheat the oven to 220°C (200°C fan). Tie the sirloin into a neat shape with kitchen string.
2. Heat a heavy-based frying pan over moderately high heat, add the oil and when hot, add the beef and brown on all sides.
3. Spray a roasting dish, just a little larger than the size of the roast, with olive oil spray and spread the onion on the base. Top the onion with most of the thyme, place the roast on top, season well with pepper, and scatter the beef with the remaining thyme.
4. Roast 15 minutes, turn the heat down to 160°C (140°C fan) and cook a further 30 minutes for rare, or 45 minutes for medium rare. Remove the meat to a warm plate, cover loosely with foil and stand 20 minutes.
5. To make the mash place the potatoes in a large saucepan of cold water and bring to the boil. Simmer uncovered for approximately 15 minutes or until potatoes are tender when pierced. Drain well in a colander then toss the potatoes back into the same saucepan and mash well with a potato masher. Pour in the milk and continue to mash until you have a light fluffy mash consistency. Season with the black pepper then set aside, covered, to keep warm.
6. Meanwhile, put the roasting pan over moderate heat, add the port and bring to a boil, scraping up any browned bits from the bottom. When the port has reduced by half, add $1/2$ cup of water and reduce by half. Strain into a clean pan, check seasoning and keep warm.
7. When ready to serve, carve the meat into thin slices. Pour any accumulated juices into the port sauce and serve with mashed potatoes and steamed vegetables.

When you want to impress, serve this roast fillet of beef to your guests or as a special treat for a family celebration. This cut is expensive, but there's absolutely no waste. The port sauce makes the whole dish festive without piling on the calories.

Nutrients per serve	
Energy (kJ)	1410kJ
Energy (cal)	338kcal
Total fat	9.0g
Saturated fat	2.9g
Monounsaturated fat	4.6g
Polyunsaturated fat	0.6g
Protein	32.6g
Carbohydrate	28.2g
Fibre	5.4g
Sodium	87mg
Cholesterol	79.5mg

Fish and leek pie with pink peppercorns

Serves **6**
Preparation time **20 minutes**
Cooking time **45 minutes**

4 large leeks, well rinsed, white and pale green parts cut into 1cm slices
1 tablespoon sunflower oil
900g firm white fish fillets, such as bream, blue-eye or snapper, cut into 2cm pieces
$^1/_4$ cup coarsely chopped flat-leaf parsley leaves
2 teaspoons pink peppercorns, coarsely chopped
8 sheets filo pastry
coarsely ground black pepper, to taste

1. Preheat the oven to 200°C (180°C fan). Lightly spray six, 1-cup capacity ovenproof dishes with oil spray.
2. Combine the leek and sunflower oil in a large non-stick frying pan and cook over moderate heat until tender, about 10 minutes, stirring frequently. Cool slightly, then combine in a bowl with the fish, parsley, pink peppercorns and plenty of coarsely ground black pepper. Spoon into the prepared dishes.
3. Lay the filo pastry on a work surface (while working, keep it between 2 damp tea towels). Cut the filo pastry into six rounds or squares of 8 layers, about 1cm larger than the dishes. Spray with oil spray between every two layers and press a stack of filo pastry on each dish. Spray the top layer with oil spray. Bake 30 minutes, or until the pastry is golden. Serve immediately.

When buying fish fillets, look for shiny firm fillets with no discoloration and a pleasant sea smell. Whole fish should also have a pleasant sea smell with a bright lustrous skin and eyes that are bright and bulging. The flesh should be firm and spring back when touched.

Nutrients per serve	
Energy (kJ)	1170kJ
Energy (cal)	279kcal
Total fat	6.8g
Saturated fat	1.6g
Monounsaturated fat	1.6g
Polyunsaturated fat	2.7g
Protein	42.3g
Carbohydrate	11.8g
Fibre	2.3g
Sodium	300mg
Cholesterol	118mg

Lentils with potato and rocket

Serves **4**
Preparation time **10 minutes**
Cooking time **70 minutes**

1 tablespoon extra virgin olive oil
2 large cloves garlic, finely chopped
$^1/_2$ teaspoon chilli flakes
400g small brown lentils
750g waxy potatoes, such as desiree, cut into 2cm cubes
$^1/_3$ cup freshly squeezed lemon juice
6 cups rocket leaves
4 black olives, preferably kalamata, stoned and quartered
lemon wedges and Italian bread, to serve
freshly ground black pepper, to taste

1. Combine the oil, garlic and chilli flakes in a casserole and cook over very low heat for 10 minutes, without colouring the garlic, stirring frequently. Add the lentils and stir in the fragrant oil for a few minutes to coat.
2. Add 6 cups (1.5 litres) water and bring to a boil. Cover and simmer gently for 20 minutes. Add the potatoes and cook, uncovered, for a further 20 minutes, or until the lentils and potatoes are tender. Add more water, if necessary.
3. Stir in the rocket, lemon juice and olives, cover and cook 5 minutes, or until the rocket has wilted. Season with pepper and serve in deep, heated plates with lemon wedges separately.

Lentils are small legumes and provide an excellent source of vegetable protein for non-meat eaters. For this dish, look for small Australian dried red lentils (brown on the outside, red inside) or otherwise ordinary brown or green lentils. Dried lentils are quick and easy to cook, but canned lentils may be used as a quicker alternative.

Nutrients per serve	
Energy (kJ)	2060kJ
Energy (cal)	493kcal
Total fat	8.0g
Saturated fat	1.0g
Monounsaturated fat	3.7g
Polyunsaturated fat	1.6g
Protein	32.7g
Carbohydrate	73.3g
Fibre	19.7g
Sodium	138mg
Cholesterol	0.0mg

Red kidney bean chilli

Serves **6**
Preparation time **20 minutes, plus overnight soaking**
Cooking time **60 minutes**

2 cups red kidney beans, soaked overnight, or quick-soaked (see tip, opposite)
1 tablespoon cumin seeds
2 teaspoons dried oregano
2 large onions, chopped
1 tablespoon peanut oil
2 cloves garlic, finely chopped
1 tablespoon mild paprika
1$^{1}/_{2}$ teaspoons chilli powder
2 cups peeled, seeded and chopped tomato, juice reserved
1 teaspoon tabasco sauce
$^{1}/_{3}$ cup chopped fresh coriander
2 tablespoons red wine vinegar
$^{1}/_{2}$ cup low fat plain yoghurt, to serve
$^{1}/_{3}$ cup low-fat ricotta, to serve

1. Drain the beans and place in a pan with fresh water to cover by 2-3cm. Bring to a boil and boil 10 minutes. Lower the heat and simmer, partially covered, until the beans are tender, about 40 minutes, then drain and set aside
2. Meanwhile, place the cumin seeds in a small non-stick frying pan and shake over moderate heat until fragrant. Add the oregano and shake the pan a further 5 seconds. Cool slightly, then pulverise the mixture in a mortar.

3. Combine the onions and oil in a non-stick pot and cook over moderate heat for 7-8 minutes, stirring frequently. Add the garlic, cumin and oregano mixture, paprika and chilli powder. Simmer gently 5 minutes, then add the tomatoes and juice, the tabasco and coriander. Simmer gently for 15 minutes, then add the beans to the mixture. Check seasoning, adding the vinegar, and more tabasco, if necessary.
4. Combine the yoghurt and ricotta in a processor and whiz until smooth. Serve the beans in heated bowls, topped with a dollop of the yoghurt mixture.

To quick-soak beans (this goes for any type of dried bean, except black-eyed beans, which have very thin skin and don't need lengthy soaking): place the beans in a pot and cover with at least twice their volume of cold water. Bring very slowly to a boil. Boil 1 minute, turn off the heat and cover the pot. Stand 1 hour – now the beans are ready to cook.

Nutrients per serve	
Energy (kJ)	658kJ
Energy (cal)	157kcal
Total fat	5.0g
Saturated fat	1.4g
Monounsaturated fat	1.7g
Polyunsaturated fat	1.2g
Protein	11.6g
Carbohydrate	15.4g
Fibre	8.5g
Sodium	87mg
Cholesterol	7.1mg

Salads

Vietnamese chicken salad with cabbage

This easy salad is vibrant with its tangy flavour, subtly supported by fish sauce and coriander. Chinese cabbage (wong nga bak) is a torpedo-shaped vegetable, perfect for salads, and almost flavourless. It is widely available in regular greengrocers.

Serves **4**
Preparation time **30 minutes**
Cooking time **5-10 minutes**

1 large red onion, halved lengthwise, thinly sliced
1 tablespoon white rice vinegar, plus 1 tablespoon extra
4 x 120g boneless, skinless chicken breasts
1 tablespoon sugar, plus 1 tablespoon extra
$1/4$ cup freshly squeezed lime juice
$1^1/2$ tablespoons fish sauce
400g chinese cabbage, very finely sliced
1 cup coriander, tough stems removed, leaves only
$1/2$ cup mint leaves, preferably vietnamese mint or spearmint
30g unsalted roasted peanuts

1. Place the onion in a bowl, add 1 tablespoon vinegar and toss well. Stand 30 minutes, drain, rinse and drain again. Combine in a bowl with 1 tablespoon sugar and set aside.
2. Meanwhile, place the chicken in one layer in a pan and add water to cover by 1cm. Remove the chicken, set aside, and bring the water to a simmer. Return the chicken to the simmering water and simmer 6 minutes or until springy to the touch. Remove the chicken from the liquid, set aside to cool, then cut into 1cm thick slices.
3. Combine the extra tablespoon sugar in another bowl with the lime juice, extra white rice vinegar and fish sauce, and stir well.
4. When ready to serve, combine the cabbage, reserved onion, chicken and lime juice dressing on a platter. Add the herbs, toss well and scatter with peanuts. Serve immediately.

Nutrients per serve	
Energy (kJ)	1170kJ
Energy (cal)	280kcal
Total fat	11.1g
Saturated fat	2.7g
Monounsaturated fat	4.6g
Polyunsaturated fat	2.1g
Protein	30.8g
Carbohydrate	13.5g
Fibre	4.1g
Sodium	666mg
Cholesterol	79.5mg

Lebanese bread salad

Serves **4**
Preparation time **20 minutes, plus 2 hours refrigeration**

4 large, vine-ripened tomatoes, cut into large cubes
4 lebanese cucumbers, peeled, seeded and cut into large cubes
1 bunch green onions, thinly sliced diagonally
1 cup coarsely chopped flat-leaf parsley
$1/3$ cup chopped fresh mint leaves
4 cups watercress, tough stems removed, well rinsed and spun dry
1 large wholemeal pita bread, halved horizontally

DRESSING
4 large cloves garlic
$1/2$ cup freshly squeezed lemon juice
1 tablespoon sumac, plus extra to sprinkle on top
1 tablespoon extra virgin olive oil
$1/2$ cup (125ml) water
freshly ground black pepper, to taste

1. Make the dressing first: crush the garlic to a paste in a mortar. Add the lemon juice and sumac, then add the oil and water in a steady trickle, whisking constantly. Season with pepper and set aside.
2. Combine the tomato, cucumber, green onion, parsley and mint in a large bowl and toss with half the dressing. Cover with plastic wrap and refrigerate for up to 2 hours.
3. Preheat a grill 30 minutes before serving.
4. Wet the bread on both sides and grill until crisp on both sides. Tear into bite-sized pieces, allow to cool slightly and toss into the salad, together with the watercress and the remaining dressing. Stand 10 minutes, then serve with a small bowl of sumac on the side.

Bread salads, popular in Mediterranean countries, range from Italian panzanella to Lebanese fattoush. The most significantly different ingredient in fattoush is "sumac", the powdered dried red berry of a Mediterranean shrub. This powder gives a lemony flavour, without having to make the dish moist with lemon juice. Sumac also gives any food it comes in contact with a reddish tinge. If sumac is not available, use extra lemon juice.

Nutrients per serve	
Energy (kJ)	735kJ
Energy (cal)	176kcal
Total fat	5.9g
Saturated fat	0.8g
Monounsaturated fat	3.4g
Polyunsaturated fat	0.6g
Protein	7.1g
Carbohydrate	22.2g
Fibre	8.9g
Sodium	194mg
Cholesterol	0.0mg

Bulgur salad with lamb fillets

Serves **6**
Preparation time **25 minutes**
Cooking time **15 minutes**

300g fine bulgur
$2^{1}/_{2}$ cups (625ml) very hot water
720g lamb fillets, trimmed of fat
freshly squeezed juice of 3 lemons
1 tablespoon mustard seed oil
freshly ground black pepper, to taste
1 cup chopped fresh flat-leaf parsley
1 cup chopped fresh mint leaves
8 green onions or spring onions, thinly sliced
1 hot red chilli, seeds removed, finely chopped
1 large zucchini, well scrubbed, cut into small cubes
2 roma tomatoes, seeded and cut into small cubes

1. Preheat the oven to 180°C (160°C fan).
2. Place the bulgur in a bowl. Stir in the hot water, cover with plastic wrap and stand until the water is absorbed and the bulgur is tender, about 20 minutes.
3. Meanwhile, spray the lamb fillets with oil. Sear them in a non-stick pan over high heat on all sides, then place the pan, in the oven for 5-8 minutes. Remove from the oven and allow to cool.
4. Drain the bulgur, removing as much water as possible. Add the juice of 3 lemons and the oil and season with pepper. Toss well. Add the herbs, onions, chilli, zucchini and tomatoes and mix well. Check seasoning, adding more lemon juice if necessary.
5. Arrange the bulgur salad on a large platter, slice the meat thinly and lay on top. Serve immediately.

Bulgur is made from wheat that has already been cooked and dried, and therefore takes little preparation. It comes in fine, medium and dry varieties. For salads such as tabbouleh, fine bulgur is recommended. Do not confuse with cracked wheat, which is uncooked. Packaged bulgur is found in most supermarkets and health food stores.

Nutrients per serve	
Energy (kJ)	1,130kJ
Energy (cal)	270kcal
Total fat	8.1g
Saturated fat	2.4g
Monounsaturated fat	3.6g
Polyunsaturated fat	1.1g
Protein	29.2g
Carbohydrate	18.9g
Fibre	5.9g
Sodium	101mg
Cholesterol	78.0mg

Beef, tomato and cucumber salad with Thai dressing

Serves **4**
Preparation time **30 minutes**
Cooking time **10 minutes**

450g sirloin steak, any visible fat removed
1 tablespoon peanut oil
500g vine-ripened tomatoes, cut into wedges
375g lebanese cucumbers, peeled and cut into 2cm pieces
1 cup coriander leaves
1 cup mint leaves

THAI DRESSING
1 lime, green peel and white pith removed, flesh cut into segments
3 small stalks lemongrass, bottom 10cm only, tough layers removed and finely sliced
$1^1/2$ tablespoons freshly squeezed lime juice
1 hot red chilli, thinly sliced on the diagonal
1 tablespoon fish sauce
3 teaspoons sugar, preferably palm sugar
3 green onions, cut into pea-sized pieces

1. Preheat a grill pan.
2. Place the beef on a plate and brush on both sides with oil. Stand for 20 minutes at room temperature. Cook the beef until rare/medium rare, about 4 minutes on the first side, then 3 minutes on the second side. Rest for 5-10 minutes and then slice.
3. Meanwhile, to make the dressing, cut the lime segments into pea-sized cubes. Finely chop enough of the tender lemongrass to make $1^1/2$ tablespoons. Combine the lemongrass, lime juice, chilli, fish sauce and sugar in a bowl and stir until sugar has dissolved. Stir in the lime and green onion and set aside.
4. Combine the tomatoes, cucumber and beef in a large bowl and toss with the dressing. Add the herbs, toss lightly, and serve immediately.

Lean red meat trimmed of all visible fat is a good source of iron. Depending on your budget and taste, other good alternatives to sirloin for a salad are fillet, scotch fillet, topside, rump, minute or blade steak. Always make sure to rest steak in a warm place for 5-10 minutes before slicing.

Nutrients per serve	
Energy (kJ)	1000kJ
Energy (cal)	240kcal
Total fat	10.4g
Saturated fat	3.2g
Monounsaturated fat	4.4g
Polyunsaturated fat	1.9g
Protein	26.7g
Carbohydrate	9.1g
Fibre	4.9g
Sodium	472mg
Cholesterol	75.5mg

Smoked fish salad with potatoes and lemon breadcrumbs

Serves **4**
Preparation time **30 minutes**
Cooking time **15 minutes**

500g salad potatoes, such as nicola or kipflers
1 tablespoon freshly squeezed lemon juice
2 tablespoons dry white wine
1 teaspoon dijon-type mustard
1 tablespoon extra virgin olive oil
1 small clove garlic, finely chopped
1 large brown shallot, finely chopped
2 tablespoons chopped flat-leaf parsley

LEMON BREADCRUMBS
1 cup fresh, fluffy breadcrumbs
1 tablespoon freshly squeezed lemon juice
grated zest of 1 lemon
1 tablespoon chopped flat-leaf parsley
2 teaspoons extra virgin olive oil

500g hot-smoked fish, such as trout or salmon
250g green beans, topped and left whole, lightly cooked in water
$1/2$ cup fresh basil leaves

1. Preheat the oven to 180°C (160°C fan).
2. Boil the potatoes in water until tender and drain. Meanwhile, combine the lemon juice, wine and mustard in a large bowl and whisk until smooth. Add the oil gradually, whisking continually. Stir in the garlic, shallot and parsley. Cut the potatoes into bite-sized pieces and stir into the dressing while potatoes are still warm. Toss well.
3. To make the lemon breadcrumbs, combine all ingredients in a large bowl, then spread on a baking sheet. Toast in the oven until golden and crisp, about 8 minutes. Allow to cool and store in an airtight container until ready to use.
4. Strip the skin off the fish and break into bite-sized pieces. Add to the potato salad, together with the beans and basil leaves. Sprinkle with lemon breadcrumbs and serve immediately.

Try to get into the habit of eating at least two fish meals every week, any type – fresh or canned. Good choices are salmon, tuna, mullet, gemfish, ling and trout. These fish are all high in beneficial marine Omega-3 fatty acids.

Nutrients per serve	
Energy (kJ)	1690kJ
Energy (cal)	404kcal
Total fat	13.9g
Saturated fat	2.5g
Monounsaturated fat	6.9g
Polyunsaturated fat	3.2g
Protein	38.0g
Carbohydrate	29.2g
Fibre	6.7g
Sodium	213mg
Cholesterol	88.3mg

Rice salad with mussels, corn and lime

Serves **4**
Preparation time **50 minutes**
Cooking time **50 minutes**

400g brown rice
24 black mussels (600g), beards removed, scrubbed if necessary
3 corn cobs, cut in half crosswise, or 250g frozen corn kernels, thawed
2 large roma tomatoes, peeled, seeded and roughly chopped
1 large clove garlic, finely chopped
$1/2$ teaspoon cumin seeds, roasted and ground
$1/4$ cup chopped red onion
$1/4$ cup chopped fresh coriander
$1/4$ cup freshly squeezed lime juice
1 tablespoon corn oil
freshly ground black pepper, to taste

1. Cook the rice in plenty of boiling water until al dente, about 30-40 minutes. Drain and set aside to cool.
2. Meanwhile, place the mussels in a large pot, cover and place over high heat. Shake the pan vigorously from time to time, until all the mussels have opened, about 6-8 minutes. Remove from pan. Discard any mussels that have not opened.
3. Plunge the corn into boiling water and cook approx 6 minutes, or until tender. Drain and when cool enough to handle, cut the kernels off the cobs with a sharp knife and transfer to a large bowl. Don't separate all the kernels.
4. Add cooled rice, tomatoes, garlic, ground cumin, onion, coriander, lime juice and oil. Toss well and season with pepper. Add mussels, removing the top shells, if desired, and toss in carefully. Cover with plastic wrap and refrigerate for 1 hour before serving.

This Mexican-inspired salad is satisfying to the max, both visually and gastronomically. Keep the corn in big pieces as they come off the cob: this makes the salad look so much more interesting. Lime juice and coriander make the whole dish sparkle with freshness.

Nutrients per serve	
Energy (kJ)	2400kJ
Energy (cal)	574kcal
Total fat	9.7g
Saturated fat	1.7g
Monounsaturated fat	2.7g
Polyunsaturated fat	4.4g
Protein	24.4g
Carbohydrate	95.4g
Fibre	7.6g
Sodium	730g
Cholesterol	43.9mg

Baby spinach salad with brazil nuts, avocado and whiting

Serves **4**
Preparation time **20 minutes**
Cooking time **5 minutes**

6 cups baby spinach leaves
$1/3$ cup coarsely chopped unsalted brazil nuts
2 tablespoons coarsely chopped dill
1 tablespoon red wine vinegar
1 small clove garlic, finely chopped
1 tablespoon avocado oil
6 green onions, thinly sliced
2 vine-ripened tomatoes, coarsely chopped
1 avocado, stoned and sliced
8 whiting fillets, about 60g each
freshly ground black pepper
4 wholegrain bread rolls

1. Combine the spinach, brazil nuts and dill in a large bowl and season with pepper.
2. Combine the vinegar and garlic in a small bowl and whisk in the oil slowly, then whisk in 2 tablespoons water. Stir in the green onions.
3. Pour the dressing over the spinach mixture and toss well. Arrange the salad on a platter, then add the tomatoes and avocado.
4. Place the whiting fillets in one layer on a plate, set the plate inside a steamer and steam 2-3 minutes or until the whiting is just cooked through. If the plate is not large enough, do this in 2 batches. Arrange the whiting on the salad. Serve immediately with wholegrain bread rolls.

Most nuts contain the healthier types of fats – polyunsaturated and monounsaturated fats. Include a variety of plain, unsalted nuts as part of healthy eating. Nuts are high in kilojoules, so if you are watching your weight, be aware of the amount of nuts you eat and how often you eat them.

Nutrients per serve	
Energy (kJ)	2289kJ
Energy (cal)	551kcal
Total fat	32.6g
Saturated fat	6.7g
Monounsaturated fat	16.1g
Polyunsaturated fat	7.7g
Protein	35.6g
Carbohydrate	27.8g
Fibre	8.1g
Sodium	385mg
Cholesterol	114.0mg

Rocket, mushroom and walnut salad with red wine dressing

Serves **4**
Preparation time **20 minutes**

60g halved unsalted walnut pieces
125g button mushrooms
4 cups rocket leaves
20g parmesan or pecorino shavings

DRESSING
1 tablespoon red wine
1 tablespoon walnut oil

1. Preheat the oven to 180°C (160°C fan).
2. Spread the walnuts on a baking sheet and toast for 8 minutes, or until fragrant. Allow to cool and then chop coarsely.
3. Wipe the mushrooms with a damp cloth, if necessary, and slice thinly. Rinse the rocket leaves, discarding any stems. Spin dry and tear into bite-sized pieces.
4. To make the dressing, place the wine in a bowl and gradually whisk in the oil, until the mixture thickens.
5. Combine the rocket leaves, mushrooms and walnuts in a bowl, pour the dressing over the salad and toss well. Stand for 10-15 minutes. Serve topped with parmesan or pecorino shavings.

There are now many great lettuce and green leafy vegetable choices you can use for salads and for sandwich fillings including cos lettuce, baby spinach, rocket, watercress, iceberg lettuce, butter lettuce and radicchio. Omitting vinegar in the dressing and substituting it with red wine means this salad is easy to match with wines. It makes a good starter for a dinner party.

Nutrients per serve	
Energy (cal)	791kJ
Energy (cal)	189kcal
Total fat	16.9g
Saturated fat	2.3g
Monounsaturated fat	5.5g
Polyunsaturated fat	7.8g
Protein	7.0g
Carbohydrate	2.5g
Fibre	2.8g
Sodium	94mg
Cholesterol	4.7mg

Potato salad with radish and cucumber

Serves **8**
Preparation time **35 minutes**
Cooking time **20 minutes**

1.5kg salad potatoes, such as nicola, kipfler or pink fir apple, scrubbed
$1/4$ cup red wine vinegar, plus $1/4$ cup extra
1 bunch radishes, trimmed and halved or quartered, depending on size
1 red onion, thinly sliced
4 lebanese cucumbers, peeled, cut in half lengthwise, seeds removed and cut into $1/2$cm slices
1 tablespoon corn oil
freshly ground black pepper

1. Cook the potatoes in boiling water until tender, about 15-20 minutes, depending on size. Drain and, when cool enough to handle, cut into bite-sized pieces. Drizzle with 3 tablespoons vinegar and set aside to cool.
2. Combine the radish, onion and cucumber in a bowl, add the extra vinegar and set aside for 30 minutes, tossing from time to time.
3. Stir the radish, onion, cucumbers and olive oil into the potatoes and season well with pepper. Serve immediately.

Have you ever seen a prettier potato salad? Using waxy potatoes gives a brilliant yellow hue, and marinating the red onion in vinegar turns it bright red. Add cucumber and radish to complete the picture. It tastes fantastic, too.

Nutrients per serve	
Energy (kJ)	674kJ
Energy (cal)	161kcal
Total fat	2.6g
Saturated fat	0.3g
Monounsaturated fat	0.6g
Polyunsaturated fat	1.2g
Protein	5.4g
Carbohydrate	27.8g
Fibre	5.0g
Sodium	26mg
Cholesterol	0.0g

Corn and avocado salad

Serves **6**
Preparation time **20 minutes**

6 corn cobs
2 red onions, chopped
2 teaspoons extra virgin olive oil
4 cloves garlic, finely chopped
2 hot red chillies, finely chopped
1$^1/_2$ large avocados, cut into bite-sized pieces
4 lebanese cucumbers, diced
freshly squeezed juice of 3 limes
1 cup coarsely chopped fresh coriander, leaves only
freshly ground black pepper, to taste

1. With a sharp knife, cut the corn off the cobs. Combine the onion and oil in a large, non-stick frying pan and cook over moderate heat until the onion is soft, about 5 minutes, stirring frequently.
2. Add the garlic and chillies and cook a further 1-2 minutes. Stir in the corn and cook 5 minutes, stirring frequently. Allow to cool to room temperature.
3. Meanwhile, in a large bowl combine the avocado and cucumber. Add the cooled corn and onion mixture and toss well. Add the lime juice and toss well. Check seasoning. Add the coriander and toss again. Season with black pepper. Serve at room temperature.

Avocados are rich in monosaturated fats and are great in salads or as a sandwich spread instead of butter. When using chillies be careful to make sure they're not too hot. Generally, the smaller the chillies and the narrower in the "shoulders", the hotter they are, so adjust the amount to suit your taste.

Nutrients per serve	
Energy (kJ)	1295kJ
Energy (cal)	312kcal
Total fat	17.4g
Saturated fat	3.4g
Monounsaturated fat	10.1g
Polyunsaturated fat	2.8g
Protein	9.0g
Carbohydrate	28.6g
Fibre	10.1g
Sodium	31mg
Cholesterol	0.0mg

Chickpea, basil and fetta salad

Serves **6**
Preparation time **20 minutes**

1 large, ripe tomato, chopped, plus 3 extra for the salad, cut into wedges
1 tablespoon extra virgin olive oil
freshly squeezed juice of 1 lemon
4 x 400g cans chickpeas, well drained, rinsed and drained again
$^1/_2$ cup ligurian or kalamata olives
1 small red onion, thinly sliced
60g reduced-fat fetta, crumbled
$^1/_3$ cup coarsely torn basil leaves
freshly ground black pepper, to taste

1. Combine the chopped tomato in a processor with the oil, lemon juice and 2 tablespoons water, and whiz until smooth.
2. Combine the remaining tomatoes in a large bowl with the chickpeas, olives, onion, fetta and basil, and season with pepper. Add the tomato dressing and toss well. Serve immediately.

Chickpeas are legumes with a nutty flavour. Dried chickpeas need to be soaked before cooking but pre-cooked ones are widely available either canned or in vacuum packs. Always rinse canned legumes very well before using.

Nutrients per serve	
Energy (kJ)	1370kJ
Energy (cal)	327kcal
Total fat	10.2g
Saturated fat	2.1g
Monounsaturated fat	3.4g
Polyunsaturated fat	3.0g
Protein	20.6g
Carbohydrate	39.0g
Fibre	14.0g
Sodium	781mg
Cholesterol	6.0mg

Vegetables

Butternut pumpkin gratin

Fresh herbs are always preferred but, if not available, you can use the dried variety. Remember the flavour is concentrated, so use only about $1/4$-$1/3$ of the amount of fresh herbs. Fresh herbs contribute extra flavour, nutrients and colour.

Serves **4**
Preparation time **30 minutes**
Cooking time **45 minutes**

2 teaspoons sunflower oil, plus 2 teaspoons extra
2 large onions, thinly sliced
1 teaspoon finely chopped fresh rosemary
1 tablespoon chopped fresh sage
6 cups 1cm butternut pumpkin cubes
$1/2$ cup plain flour
2 tablespoons chopped flat-leaf parsley
30g grated reduced-fat cheddar cheese
$1/2$ cup plus 1 tablespoon (150ml) low-fat milk
1 cup fresh, fluffy breadcrumbs
freshly ground black pepper, to taste

1. Preheat the oven to 190°C (170°C fan). Spray an 8-cup gratin dish lightly with olive oil spray.
2. Combine 2 teaspoons oil, onions, rosemary and sage in a large non-stick frying pan and cook over moderate heat until the onions start to caramelise, about 15 minutes, stirring frequently. Season with pepper and spread in the prepared dish.
3. Toss the pumpkin in the flour and discard the excess. Add the extra 2 teaspoons oil to the frying pan. Add the pumpkin to the pan and cook until browning, about 7 minutes, tossing frequently. Add the parsley, season with plenty of pepper and cook a further 1 minute.
4. Top the onions with the pumpkin, scatter with the cheese and pour over the milk. Cover with foil and bake 20 minutes, then remove the foil and scatter with the breadcrumbs. Bake until the top is brown and the liquid has been absorbed, about a further 20-25 minutes.

Nutrients per serve	
Energy (kJ)	1260kJ
Energy (cal)	301kcal
Total fat	8.6g
Saturated fat	2.5g
Monounsaturated fat	2.2g
Polyunsaturated fat	3.4g
Protein	13.4g
Carbohydrate	42.5g
Fibre	4.9g
Sodium	167mg
Cholesterol	7.2mg

Braised mushrooms and potatoes

Serves **6**
Preparation time **5 minutes**
Cooking time **35 minutes**

20g porcini mushrooms
1.5kg kipfler potatoes
1 tablespoon extra virgin olive oil
4 large cloves garlic, finely chopped
500g field mushrooms, cleaned and cut into 1cm slices
2 tablespoons chopped flat-leaf parsley
freshly ground black pepper, to taste

1. Place the porcini mushrooms in a small bowl and cover with boiling water. Leave 20 minutes or until needed. Line a sieve with a damp paper towel and drain the porcini, reserving the soaking water. Check the porcini pieces for grit and set aside.
2. Meanwhile, bring a large pot of water to a boil and cook potatoes until tender, about 15 minutes. Set aside to cool slightly then slice on the diagonal in $1/2$cm thick slices
3. Combine the oil and garlic in a large non-stick pan and cook over moderately low heat until the garlic is fragrant, about 1 minute. Add the field mushrooms, turn up the heat and cook 5 minutes, stirring frequently. Stir in the parsley and season with pepper. Set aside.
4. Combine the potatoes with the field mushrooms, the reserved porcini and approximately half a cup of the porcini soaking water. Toss gently, and cook over low heat for 10 minutes.

Who doesn't love potatoes? This wonderful new take on everyone's favourite will give added variety and flavour to your next family meal or barbecue.

Nutrients per serve	
Energy (kJ)	883kJ
Energy (cal)	211kcal
Total fat	3.6g
Saturated fat	0.4g
Monounsaturated fat	2.2g
Polyunsaturated fat	0.3g
Protein	9.2g
Carbohydrate	34.4g
Fibre	6.5g
Sodium	15mg
Cholesterol	0.0mg

Balsamic roast vegetables

Serves **6**
Preparation time **20 minutes**
Cooking time **40 minutes**

375g sweet potato, peeled and cut into 4cm chunks
375g red onion, cut through the root into 2cm wedges
375g large carrots, cut into 4cm chunks
375g large zucchini, cut into 4cm chunks
500g waxy potatoes, such as nicola, cut into 4cm chunks
12 cloves garlic, peeled
$1/2$ cup thyme sprigs
2 tablespoons extra virgin olive oil
2 tablespoons balsamic vinegar
freshly ground black pepper, to taste

1. Preheat the oven to 220°C (200°C fan).
2. Combine the sweet potato, onion, carrots, zucchini, waxy potatoes and garlic in a large bowl. Add the thyme sprigs, oil and balsamic vinegar and season with plenty of black pepper.
3. Toss the vegetables well and spread them in a single layer in a large baking dish. Use two baking dishes if necessary. Roast until the vegetables are cooked through and starting to brown on the edges, about 40 minutes. Serve immediately.

When buying vegetables, try to incorporate as many colours of the rainbow as possible. Not only because they look so good together, but also because they all contribute different anti-oxidants to your meals. Other vegetables suitable for a roast are pumpkin with skin on, capsicum, squash, parsnips, marrow, tomato and cauliflower.

Nutrients per serve

Energy (kJ)	834kJ
Energy (cal)	199kcal
Total fat	6.6g
Saturated fat	0.9g
Monounsaturated fat	4.3g
Polyunsaturated fat	0.6g
Protein	5.9g
Carbohydrate	28.5g
Fibre	7.8g
Sodium	49mg
Cholesterol	0.0mg

Desserts

Summer puddings

Serves **6**
Preparation time **20 minutes plus overnight setting in the fridge**
Cooking time **5 minutes**

    1kg mixed berries
$1/4$ **cup caster sugar**
$1/2$ **loaf sliced sandwich bread, crusts removed and flattened with a rolling pin**

1. Combine berries and sugar in a pan and slowly bring to the boil, stirring gently until sugar has dissolved and juices are plentiful, adding more sugar if necessary. Drain in a colander set over a bowl to catch the juices. Cool the fruit and reserve the juices.
2. Cut 12 circles of the bread to fit the bottom and tops of 6 x $3/4$ cup (185ml) moulds. Dip circles for bottoms into juice and place in the moulds. Cut remaining bread slices into halves for the sides of the mould.
3. Dip the strips in the juice to line sides and fit in the moulds, slightly overlapping. Fill with berry mixture and top with the reserved circles, dipped in juice. Reserve any remaining berries and juice, and puree to serve with puddings.
4. Place the moulds in a dish (to catch any juices), and cover with plastic wrap. Place another dish or baking sheet on top and put in the fridge, with a few heavy cans or weights on top. Leave at least 4 hours, or preferably overnight. Run a knife around the inside of moulds to release.

This evergreen pudding is actually good for you! Fruits, along with vegetables, legumes, wholegrain bread and cereals, are high in fibre and, when eaten every day, these foods may help to lower risk of heart disease and also to keep you regular.

Nutrients per serve	
Energy (kJ)	558kJ
Energy (cal)	133kcal
Total fat	1.1g
Saturated fat	0.1g
Monounsaturated fat	0.2g
Polyunsaturated fat	0.3g
Protein	5.7g
Carbohydrate	25.3g
Fibre	5.6g
Sodium	160mg
Cholesterol	0.0mg

Strawberry souffle

Serves **6**
Preparation time **20 minutes**
Cooking time **20-25 minutes**

16 large strawberries, about 600g
$^1/_4$ cup caster sugar, plus 1 tablespoon extra, to coat the ramekins
1 tablespoon Grand Marnier or Cointreau
4 large eggwhites
$^1/_8$ teaspoon cream of tartar

1. Preheat the oven to 180°C (160°C fan). Spray 6 x $^3/_4$ cup (185ml) ramekins with oil spray. Add a little of the sugar to one ramekin and rotate in your hands to coat the inside. Add any remaining sugar to the next ramekin and repeat the procedure until all the ramekins have been coated with sugar. Place the dishes on a baking tray and place another baking tray in the oven to heat.

2. Rinse the strawberries, hull and slice them. Combine the strawberries in a pan with 2 tablespoons of the sugar and cook over moderate heat until the berries are almost a jam consistency, approximately 15 minutes. Puree them in a processor and place in a large bowl. Stir in the Grand Marnier or Cointreau.

3. In another clean, dry bowl beat the eggwhites until foamy. Add the cream of tartar and slowly beat in the remaining 1 tablespoon of the sugar until the whites are glossy with stiff peaks. Add $^1/_4$ of the eggwhites to the strawberries and mix well, then add the remaining eggwhites and fold in gently.

4. Spoon souffle mixture into the prepared ramekins. Place the baking tray on top of the preheated baking tray and bake 20-25 minutes, or until well risen and golden. Serve immediately.

When you bring a souffle to the table at the end of the meal, people will think you're a crash-hot cook. In reality nothing could be simpler, the secret is in the beating of the eggwhites: they should just hold stiff peaks – they may gently bend over, but not droop. Remember, you're not making meringue – the whites should still be soft enough to fold into the fruit base. Once the whites are over-beaten, they become dry and you won't be able to fold them in.

Nutrients per serve	
Energy (kJ)	342kJ
Energy (cal)	82kcal
Total fat	0.1g
Saturated fat	0.0g
Monounsaturated fat	0.0g
Polyunsaturated fat	0.0g
Protein	3.6g
Carbohydrate	15.2g
Fibre	1.6g
Sodium	53mg
Cholesterol	0.0mg

Mangoes with hot brown sugar syrup and lemon ricotta cream

Serves **4**
Preparation time **15 minutes**
Cooking time **5 minutes**

4 large mangoes, unpeeled and sliced

HOT BROWN SUGAR SYRUP
$1/4$ cup brown sugar
$1/2$ cup (125ml) water

LEMON RICOTTA CREAM
$1/2$ cup low-fat ricotta
$1/4$ cup low-fat plain yoghurt
1 tablespoon freshly squeezed lemon juice

1. Place the mangoes on a plate and refrigerate.
2. To make the hot brown sugar syrup, combine the sugar and water in a pan and bring to a boil. Cook until syrupy, about 5 minutes.
3. To make the lemon ricotta cream, combine the ricotta, yoghurt and lemon juice in a processor and whiz until smooth.
4. Serve the fruit straight from the fridge, with the hot syrup poured over and the lemon ricotta cream on the side.

Ricotta is a moist, delicate cheese, which is an ideal substitute for cream cheese when reducing the saturated fat content in recipes. Reduced-fat ricotta contains about five per cent fat and has less salt than regular cheese.

Nutrients per serve	
Energy (kJ)	923kJ
Energy (cal)	221kcal
Total fat	3.3g
Saturated fat	1.8g
Monounsaturated fat	0.8g
Polyunsaturated fat	0.1g
Protein	6.4g
Carbohydrate	41.7g
Fibre	3.1g
Sodium	77mg
Cholesterol	14.4mg

Baked winter fruits

Serves **6**
Preparation time **10 minutes**
Cooking time **60 minutes**

1 cup (250ml) red wine
1 cinnamon stick
2 bay leaves
500g apples, cored and quartered
500g pears, cored and quartered
15 dates, halved and stoned
$1/2$ cup brown sugar, loosely packed
2 cups low-fat yoghurt, to serve

1. Preheat the oven to 180°C (160°C fan).
2. Combine the wine, cinnamon and bay leaves in a small pan and bring to a boil. Stand a few minutes.
3. Combine the apples, pears and dates in an ovenproof dish and sprinkle with the brown sugar.
4. Pour the red wine mixture over the fruit. Bake 60 minutes or until the fruit is tender, basting from time to time. Serve hot, warm or at room temperature, with low-fat yoghurt.

Fruit-based desserts are a great option as they are often lower in saturated fat and higher in fibre. With the variety of fresh, canned (in water or natural juice), or dried fruits available, there are so many great choices!

Nutrients per serve	
Energy (kJ)	994kJ
Energy (cal)	238kcal
Total fat	0.4g
Saturated fat	0.1g
Monounsaturated fat	0.1g
Polyunsaturated fat	0.0g
Protein	5.8g
Carbohydrate	46.5g
Fibre	3.4g
Sodium	79mg
Cholesterol	5.2mg

Nectarines with meringue topping

Serves **4**
Preparation time **15 minutes**
Cooking time **30 minutes**

$1/4$ cup caster sugar, plus 1 tablespoon extra for the dish, plus 1 tablespoon extra
  for the fruit
1kg ripe nectarines, washed and dried, cut in half and stones removed
2 large eggwhites
grated rind of $1/2$ lemon

1. Preheat the oven to 180°C (160°C fan). Spray a baking dish lightly with oil and sprinkle with 1 tablespoon extra sugar.
2. Arrange the nectarines in the dish, cut sides up, and sprinkle with another 1 tablespoon sugar. Bake 10 minutes.
3. Meanwhile, in a clean, dry bowl beat the eggwhites until soft peaks form. Gradually add half of $1/4$ cup sugar, while beating, until stiff peaks form. Fold in the remaining sugar and lemon rind.
4. Spoon a couple of tablespoons of meringue into each nectarine half then bake for 15-20 minutes or until the meringue is set and golden. Serve immediately.

When nectarines are not available, you can replace them with nectareds, peaches, plums or apricots. In winter you can still make this dish – simply use canned nectarines, peaches, plums or apricots.

Nutrients per serve

Energy (kJ)	675kJ
Energy (cal)	161kcal
Total fat	0.0g
Saturated fat	0.0g
Monounsaturated fat	0.0g
Polyunsaturated fat	0.0g
Protein	4.4g
Carbohydrate	37.4g
Fibre	4.8g
Sodium	40mg
Cholesterol	0.0mg

Vanilla rice pudding

Serves **4**
Preparation time **15 minutes**
Cooking time **40 minutes**

120g pudding rice, such as arborio or calrose
4 cups (1 litre) skim milk, plus a little extra for cornflour paste, plus $^1/_4$ cup, extra
$^1/_2$ cup (90g) caster sugar
2 strips lemon zest
$1^1/_2$ teaspoons cornflour
$^1/_2$ teaspoon vanilla essence
2 egg yolks
500g fresh berries, to serve

1. Bring a large pot of water to a boil, add the rice and cook 5 minutes. Drain and return to the pan. Add the milk, sugar and lemon zest and bring to a boil. Simmer very slowly for 40 minutes, or until the pudding is thick and most of the milk has been absorbed. Discard the lemon zest.
2. Use a little extra milk to make the cornflour into a paste and stir this into the rice pudding, together with the vanilla. Cook a further 5 minutes, then remove from the heat.
3. Stir in the egg yolk and the extra milk. This pudding may be served in small bowls, warm, at room temperature or chilled. Serve with berries in season.

Replacing full cream dairy products, such as milk and yoghurt, with low- or reduced-fat varieties, provides a product that's packed full of nutrition. Not only are they low in saturated fat, but most contain more calcium than the full-fat varieties.

Nutrients per serve	
Energy (kJ)	976kJ
Energy (cal)	233kcal
Total fat	1.8g
Saturated fat	0.7g
Monounsaturated fat	0.6g
Polyunsaturated fat	0.2g
Protein	13.6g
Carbohydrate	41.2g
Fibre	3.1g
Sodium	130mg
Cholesterol	61.4mg

Fresh strawberry jellies

Serves **6**
Preparation time **20 minutes plus overnight setting**

750g strawberries, hulled and pureed
freshly squeezed juice of $^1/_2$ lemon
2 tablespoons powdered gelatine
$^1/_4$ cup cold water, plus 100ml extra
$^1/_3$ cup caster sugar

1. Lightly spray six 150ml moulds with oil.
2. Place the pureed strawberries in a bowl and stir in the lemon juice.
3. Sprinkle the gelatine over $^1/_4$ cup water in a small bowl. Place the bowl in a shallow pan, with water coming up halfway. Bring the water in the pan to a simmer and stir the gelatine mixture until it is absolutely clear. Keep warm in the pan.
4. In another pan bring the remaining 100ml water to a boil and add the sugar. Stir until the sugar has dissolved. Add this mixture to the strawberries, together with the reserved gelatine mixture. Pour into the prepared moulds and refrigerate overnight.
5. Turn out of the moulds and serve immediately.

These jellies shimmer like jewels on the plate and they're so easy to make. Nothing but the goodness of fresh fruit, these are just the thing to finish a heavy meal without weighing you down. Instead of strawberries you'll have equally successful results with raspberries, redcurrants, blueberries or blackberries.

Nutrients per serve

Energy (kJ)	349kJ
Energy (cal)	84kcal
Total fat	0.1g
Saturated fat	0.0g
Monounsaturated fat	0.0g
Polyunsaturated fat	0.0g
Protein	5.7g
Carbohydrate	14.9g
Fibre	2.7g
Sodium	22mg
Cholesterol	0.0mg

Baking

Chocolate banana cake

You don't always have to have fresh fruits on hand for baking – make a habit of freezing some when in season, and therefore plentiful and cheap. Freeze bananas in their skin – they will turn black in the freezer but the inside fruit will be white, and as creamy as usual. Pureed cooked fruit adds flavour, sweetness and a moist texture to cakes and muffins.

Serves **8-10**
Preparation time **15 minutes**
Cooking time **1 hour**

1 cup freshly squeezed orange juice
2 very ripe bananas, peeled
150g wholemeal self-raising flour
150g white self-raising flour
1 teaspoon baking powder
30g dark chocolate, finely chopped
2 eggwhites
3/4 cup (150g) firmly packed soft brown sugar

1. Preheat the oven to 160°C (140°C fan). Line a loaf tin with baking paper and spray lightly with oil spray.
2. Combine the orange juice and bananas in a processor and whiz until smooth. Transfer to a large bowl.
3. Sift together the flours and baking powder, add the chocolate and stir into the banana mixture. Whisk a few minutes.
4. Whisk the eggwhites until stiff peaks form, add the sugar little by little, whisking after each addition. Fold the eggwhite mixture into the flour mixture, until no white streaks remain. Spoon the mixture into the prepared tin and level the top. Bake 1 hour, or until a skewer comes out clean when tested.
5. Cool in the tin on a wire rack for 5 minutes. Loosen with a sharp knife around the sides and turn out. Cool completely on the wire rack, then store, wrapped in foil, in an airtight container. Best after 1 day.

Nutrients per serve	
Energy (kJ)	830kJ
Energy (cal)	202kcal
Total fat	1.4g
Saturated fat	0.6g
Monounsaturated fat	0.3g
Polyunsaturated fat	0.3g
Protein	4.7g
Carbohydrate	42.4g
Fibre	3.0g
Sodium	254mg
Cholesterol	0.0mg

Pear tart with raspberries

Serves **6**
Preparation time **20 minutes**
Cooking time **30 minutes**

3 teaspoons extra light olive oil
800g pears (about 4 medium), peeled, cored and quartered
cooking oil spray
6 sheets filo pastry
30g unsalted hazelnuts, lightly toasted and finely chopped
1 punnet raspberries
1 teaspoon coarse sugar

1. Preheat the oven to 180°C (160°C fan).
2. Heat the oil in a large non-stick frying pan. Add the pears and cook over moderately
high heat until the pears are golden on all sides and releasing some of their juices. Set aside
on paper towels.
3. Lightly spray a 25cm pie dish, and place one sheet of filo pastry in the dish. Lay another
sheet of filo pastry on an angle on top of the first sheet of the filo, spray lightly with oil and
sprinkle with $^1/_3$ of the hazelnuts. Keep layering the filo, staggering them, spraying oil lightly
between every second sheet and sprinkling with hazelnuts.
4. Place the pears in the pastry and scatter with raspberries. Fold the overhanging filo pastry
back over the fruit, spray with oil and scatter with hazelnuts and sugar. Bake for 30 minutes, or
until the filo pastry is golden. Serve warm or at room temperature.

The hazelnuts add extra crunch and delicious flavour. Walnuts, almonds or pecans are good alternatives. Raspberries are at their best when fresh but, when frozen, they are nearly as good and bring a touch of summer year round. You could use strawberries or blueberries instead.

Nutrients per serve	
Energy (KJ)	741kJ
Energy (cal)	177kcal
Total fat	5.9g
Saturated fat	0.5g
Monounsaturated fat	4.2g
Polyunsaturated fat	0.7g
Protein	2.8g
Carbohydrate	28.9g
Fibre	5.9g
Sodium	98mg
Cholesterol	0.0mg

Polenta and dried apricot muffins

Serves **12**
Preparation time **15 minutes**
Cooking time **30 minutes**

80g fine cornmeal, plus 80g extra
140g plain flour
$1/2$ teaspoon bicarb soda
100g dried apricots, coarsely chopped
3 eggwhites, plus 2 eggwhites, extra
2 tablespoons honey
275ml buttermilk
1 cup water
1 teaspoon vanilla essence

1. Preheat the oven to 190°C (170°C fan). Line a non-stick 12-cup muffin tray with paper muffin cases.
2. Combine 80g of the fine cornmeal, flour and bicarb soda in a sieve and sift into a bowl. Mix through the dried apricots and set aside.
3. Beat the 3 eggwhites until foamy and stir in the honey and buttermilk.
4. Bring the water to a boil in a non-stick pan, pour in the extra 80g cornmeal, whisking constantly. Stir with a wooden spoon until the mixture is very smooth and pulls away from the sides of the pan. Scrape the mixture into a large bowl.
5. Add the eggwhite and buttermilk mixture and stir in the vanilla essence. Fold the flour and dried apricot mixture into the cooked cornmeal.
6. In a clean, dry bowl beat the extra 2 eggwhites until stiff peaks form. Stir 2 tablespoons into the muffin mixture, then gently fold in the rest of the eggwhites, without over-mixing. Divide the mixture among the lined muffin cups making sure to fill well, then bake 25 minutes or until well risen and golden. The muffins are cooked when a testing skewer comes out clean when tested.
7. Turn the muffins in their paper cups out off the tin and cool on a wire rack.

Not many people can resist a muffin, and though these delicious morsels make a fabulous start to the day, they're equally good at teatime. Buttermilk makes them extra moist. Buttermilk is not as high in kilojoules as it may sound: it used to be the liquid left over once the butter was churned. These days it's made by adding bacteria to non-fat or low-fat milk, making it slightly thicker, with a tangy flavour. It's especially good in baking.

Nutrients per serve	
Energy (kJ)	568kJ
Energy (cal)	136kcal
Total fat	0.9g
Saturated fat	0.4g
Monounsaturated fat	0.3g
Polyunsaturated fat	0.1g
Protein	5.1g
Carbohydrate	26.7g
Fibre	1.6g
Sodium	63mg
Cholesterol	2.1mg

Chocolate berry slice

Makes **18 squares**
Preparation time **15 minutes**
Cooking time **45 minutes**

3 eggs
75ml sunflower oil
200ml buttermilk
$^3/_4$ cup caster sugar
220g self-raising flour
$^1/_3$ cup cocoa powder
$^1/_2$ teaspoon bicarb soda
250g fresh or frozen raspberries, strawberries or blueberries (if using frozen make sure
    they are unthawed) plus
250g berries extra, to serve
750g low-fat yoghurt

1. Preheat the oven to 170°C (150°C fan) and lightly spray a 20 x 25cm brownie tin with oil.
2. Using a hand-held beater, beat together the eggs, oil, buttermilk and sugar in a mixing bowl
until well combined.
3. In a separate bowl sift together the flour, cocoa powder and bicarb soda. Fold into the egg
mixture then carefully add 250g of the raspberries and fold to combine.
4. Pour the mixture into the prepared tin and bake on the centre shelf of the preheated oven
for approximately 45 minutes or until a cake skewer comes out clean when inserted into
the middle of the slice. Remove from the oven and allow to cool for 10 minutes.
5. Cut into 18 squares then carefully transfer to a wire rack to cool completely.
6. Serve with the extra berries and a dollop of low-fat yoghurt.

Who would have thought you could eat this luscious chocolate cake and still maintain your healthy lifestyle. Make sure you use a good quality cocoa powder, not drinking chocolate, and the result will be worthy of a grand celebration, be it for a birthday, a christening or an end-of-term party.

Nutrients per serve	
Energy (kJ)	689kJ
Energy (cal)	167kcal
Total fat	6.1g
Saturated fat	1.3g
Monounsaturated fat	1.7g
Polyunsaturated fat	2.7g
Protein	6.4g
Carbohydrate	20.6g
Fibre	2.0g
Sodium	144mg
Cholesterol	33.1mg

Fruit mince tarts

Makes **12**
Preparation time **20 minutes**
Cooking time **25 minutes**

$1^1/_2$ cups sundried mixed fruit
$^1/_2$ cup dried figs
1 pear, peeled and finely chopped
2 tablespoons chopped pecan nuts
1 teaspoon grated orange rind
1 teaspoon grated lemon rind
1 teaspoon ground cinnamon
2 tablespoons rum

PASTRY
2 cups plain flour
1 cup almond meal
2 tablespoons icing sugar (plus a tablespoon extra for dusting)
60g polyunsaturated margarine
1 egg, plus a beaten eggwhite (for brushing the pastry)
$^1/_3$ cup iced water

1. Preheat the oven to 180°C (160°C fan) and lightly spray 12 x $^1/_2$ cup capacity muffin tins.
2. Mix the dried fruit, pear, pecan nuts, orange and lemon rinds, ground cinnamon and rum in a bowl and allow to macerate overnight if possible, or while you make the pastry.
3. To make the pastry place all of the pastry ingredients except the iced water in the bowl of a food processor, and pulse until the consistency of fine breadcrumbs. With the motor running add the iced water and process until the mixture comes together to form a ball.
4. Transfer the pastry on to a lightly floured surface and knead for a few minutes. Roll the pastry out until it is 3mm thick. Cut 12 x 8cm rounds from the pastry, and 12 star shapes using a star-shaped biscuit cutter.
5. Line the bases of the muffin tins with the pastry circles and spoon a tablespoon of the fruit mince mixture into each pastry case. Place a pastry star on top and brush each tart with the beaten eggwhite. Bake in the preheated oven for approximately 30 minutes or until golden and cooked. Allow the tarts to cool in the tins for 10 minutes before transferring to a wire rack to cool completely. When cold, dust the tarts with the extra icing sugar and serve.

It's not really Christmas without fruit mince tarts and these festive little delicacies will definitely hit the mark. Instead of the pastry recipe used here, you could also try making them with filo or canola-based puff pastry.

Nutrients per serve	
Energy (kJ)	1190kJ
Energy (cal)	285kcal
Total fat	11.1g
Saturated fat	1.3g
Monounsaturated fat	5.5g
Polyunsaturated fat	3.5g
Protein	6.0g
Carbohydrate	39.6g
Fibre	4.4g
Sodium	69mg
Cholesterol	15.1mg

Tuscan apple cake

Serves **12**
Preparation time **15 minutes**
Cooking time **45 minutes**

2 large eggs
$^1/_4$ cup caster sugar
200g plain flour
2 teaspoons baking powder
2 teaspoons grated lemon zest
$^2/_3$ cup low-fat milk
800g golden delicious apples, peeled, cored and thinly sliced
$^1/_4$ cup demerara sugar

1. Preheat the oven to 180°C (160°C fan). Lightly spray a non-stick, 22cm springform tin with oil. Dust with a little flour, shaking out excess. Set aside.
2. In a large bowl, whisk the eggs until pale, add $^1/_4$ cup of the sugar and and beat in well. Whisk in the flour, baking powder and lemon zest, then slowly whisk in the milk. Set aside for 15 minutes.
3. Pour the batter into the prepared tin, then arrange the apples on top, pressing down so all the apples fit. Sprinkle the top with demerara sugar and bake 45 minutes or until a testing skewer comes out clean.
4. Cool in the tin on a wire rack for 5 minutes. Run a knife around the edge and release the spring. Place on a platter and serve warm or at room temperature. Dust with icing sugar, if you like.

The top of this apple cake is sprinkled with demerara sugar. This sugar is widely available in supermarkets. Demerara is a raw brown sugar, coated with a little molasses for colour and flavour. The size of the granules – between coffee crystals and caster sugar – means they don't melt when baking, giving a crunchy top.

Nutrients per serve	
Energy (kJ)	698kJ
Energy (cal)	167kcal
Total fat	1.3g
Saturated fat	0.4g
Monounsaturated fat	0.5g
Polyunsaturated fat	0.2g
Protein	4.1g
Carbohydrate	35.2g
Fibre	3.0g
Sodium	62mg
Cholesterol	37.4mg

Index

Glossary

Carbohydrates are found mainly in plant foods and supply the body with kilojoules which are used for energy. Carbohydrate sources include cereal foods (bread, breakfast cereals, rice, pasta, couscous, polenta, burghal and oats), fruit, some vegetables (potato, sweet corn, sweet potato and yam) and legumes/pulses (dried peas, beans, lentils). Some dairy and soy products (soy beverages, yoghurt, custard) also provide carbohydrates. Carbohydrate is also found in sugar and honey.

Cholesterol may be one of two different types:

a) Blood cholesterol is a fatty substance normally produced by the body and carried by the blood. There are two different types: LDL cholesterol (also known as "bad" cholesterol) and HDL cholesterol (also known as "good" cholesterol). High levels of LDL cholesterol and low levels of HDL cholesterol in the blood are risk factors for heart disease and atherosclerosis.

b) Dietary cholesterol is found only in animal foods (offal, fatty meats and poultry, eggs, full-fat milk, full-fat cheese, and so on). A lot of dietary cholesterol may raise blood cholesterol, particularly in people with a high risk of developing heart disease. However, cholesterol in food does not raise cholesterol in the blood to the same extent as saturated and trans fats. Replacing saturated fats with polyunsaturated and monounsaturated fats is the most effective way to help lower your blood cholesterol level.

Dietary fibre is found only in plant foods. Plant foods contain a mixture of different types of fibre in varying proportions. For this reason, make sure each meal contains lots of vegetables, fruit, grain-based foods including wholegrain breads, rice, pasta, breakfast cereals, and legumes, seeds and nuts.

Energy is the amount of kilojoules (or Calories) eaten or used up by the body through day-to-day activities. A high-energy food is a food that is high in kilojoules.

Folic acid (folate) is a B vitamin found naturally in most plant foods, especially green leafy and other vegetables (spinach, brussels sprouts, broccoli, asparagus, leek, cauliflower and cabbage), fruit (oranges, strawberries, bananas), wholegrain breads, cereals, legumes (peas, dried beans, lentils), nuts and yeast extract. It can also be added to products such as some breads and breakfast cereals.

Hypertension is another word for high blood pressure. High blood pressure is a major risk factor for heart disease.

Iron is a mineral present in animal foods such as red meats, poultry and seafood. It is also found in plant foods such as cereals, fruit, vegetables and legumes, however it is less easily absorbed.

Kilojoule (kJ) is a term for the amount of energy released when a food is burned for fuel in the body or the amount of energy burnt by the body during physical activity. The old Imperial term for this energy is Calorie. (4.2 kilojoules = 1 Calorie.)

Legumes are dried beans, peas and lentils, which are also known as pulses. Examples include kidney beans, chickpeas, split peas and baked beans.

Monounsaturated fat is a type of fat that may help to lower blood cholesterol when eaten in place of saturated fat. Sources include monounsaturated margarine spreads; olive, canola and peanut oils; avocado; nuts and seeds.

Omega-3 fats (or omega-3 fatty acids) are a type of polyunsaturated fat found commonly in fish and certain plant-based foods. These types of fats have been shown to be beneficial in helping to reduce your risk of heart disease. Omega-3 fats can be divided into two groups:

a) EPA (Eicosapentaenoic acid) and DHA (Docosahexaenoic acid) are types of Omega-3 polyunsaturated fats mainly found in oily fish such as salmon, sardines, mackarel, trevally and tuna.

b) ALA (Alpha Linolenic Acid) is a different type of Omega-3 polyunsaturated fat. Canola and soybean oils, linseeds (flaxseeds) and walnuts are high in ALA.

Polyunsaturated fat is a type of fat that may help to lower blood cholesterol and triglycerides when eaten in place of saturated fat. Sources include polyunsaturated margarine spreads; corn, safflower, soybean and sunflower oils; deep sea oily fish; shellfish; nuts and seeds.

Protein is found in both animal and plant foods and supplies the body with kilojoules and amino acids necessary for the growth, maintenance and repair of body tissue.

- Animal sources of protein include red and white meat, eggs and dairy products.
- Plant sources of protein include cereal foods (bread, breakfast cereals, rice, pasta, couscous, polenta, burghal and oats), nuts, legumes/pulses (dried or canned peas and beans including split peas, haricot and kidney beans, baked beans, three bean mix and lentils) and some soy products (tofu, tempeh, cheese, soy beverages, yoghurt, custard).

Saturated fat is the type of fat that raises blood cholesterol levels. To reduce your risk of heart disease, it's important to reduce your intake of foods high in saturated fats. Foods high in saturated fat include fatty meats, full-fat dairy products, butter, two vegetable oils (coconut and palm oil), most deep-fried takeaways and commercially baked products such as biscuits and pastries.

Sodium in our food comes mainly from added salt, either in processed food or added in cooking. Lowering your sodium intake may help control blood pressure.

Recipe notes & imperial/metric conversion chart

Each recipe has been carefully analysed by the Heart Foundation to ensure it is in line with our healthy eating philosophy and meets our nutrition guidelines regarding fat (particularly type of fat), kilojoules, sodium and fibre.

We provide you with the nutrition profile of each recipe in a "nutrients per serve" table.

The nutrition information provided is based on the recommended serving size per recipe, which can be found above the ingredient list for each recipe.

Where individual items or a large number of serves are mentioned (such as makes 12 muffins), the analysis is based on one item, serve or portion: in this example, one muffin.

Energy per serve is expressed as both kilojoules (kJ) and Calories (Cal). Other nutrients are in grams (g) or milligrams (mg). Accompaniments, garnishes, optional ingredients and "to taste" ingredients are not included in the nutritional analysis, however the "to serve" suggestions are included.

Preparation and cooking times are based on estimates of the time it would take a person who is familiar with cooking, but not an expert. The times may vary according to your experience.

Metric cup and spoon sizes

Measurements used in this book refer to the standard metric cup and spoon sets approved by Standards Australia.

A basic metric cup set consists of:
  1 cup, $1/2$ cup, $1/3$ cup and $1/4$ cup sizes,
The basic spoon set comprises
  1 tablespoon, 1 teaspoon, $1/2$ teaspoon, $1/4$ teaspoon.

Cup	Spoon
$1/4$ cup = 60 ml	$1/4$ teaspoon = 1.25 ml
$1/3$ cup = 80 ml	$1/2$ teaspoon = 2.5 ml
$1/2$ cup = 125 ml	1 teaspoon = 5 ml
1 cup = 250 ml	1 tablespoon = 20 ml

Mass (weight) – approximate conversion for cookery purposes

Imperial	Metric	Imperial	Metric
$1/2$oz	15g	10oz	315g
1oz	30g	11oz	345g
2oz	60g	12oz ($3/4$ lb)	375g
3oz	90g	13oz	410g
4oz ($1/4$ lb)	125g	14oz	440g
5oz	155g	15oz	470g
6oz	185g	16oz (1 lb)	500g (0. 5kg)
7oz	220g	24oz ($1^1/2$ lb)	750g
8oz ($1/2$ lb)	250g	32oz (2 1b)	1000g (1 kg)
9oz	280g	3 lb	1500g (1.5kg)

Liquids

Imperial	Metric	Metric
1 fl oz	-	30 ml
2 fl oz	$1/4$ cup	60 ml
3 fl oz	-	100 ml
4 fl oz	$1/2$ cup	125 ml
5 fl oz	-	150 ml
6 fl oz	$3/4$ cup	200 ml
8 fl oz	1 cup	250 ml
10 fl oz	$1^1/4$ cups	300 ml
12 fl oz	$1^1/2$ cups	375 ml
14 fl oz	$1^3/4$ cups	425 ml
15 fl oz	-	475 ml
16 fl oz	2 cups	500 ml
20 fl oz (1 pint)	$2^1/2$ cups	600 ml

Oven temperatures

Oven	Fahrenheit	Celsius
Very slow	250	120
Slow	275-300	140-150
Moderately slow	325	160
Moderate	350	180
Moderately hot	375	190
Hot	400-450	200-230
Very hot	475-500	250-260

Note: Set fan oven at approximately 20° Celsius below the stated temperature.

Heart Foundation

The Heart Foundation is the leading national heart health charity fighting to improve and save lives from cardiovascular disease (includes heart disease, stroke and blood vessel disease).

Cardiovascular disease is the leading cause of death in Australia and kills more than 50,000 Australians each year – that's one Australian life lost every 10 minutes. It is the greatest source of premature death and disability in the Australian community.

The money the Heart Foundation raises through donations, sales and gifts in wills is used to improve the heart health of Australians and reduce death from cardiovascular disease by:

- **Funding research:** the Heart Foundation promotes and funds research to gain knowledge about heart disease to help prevent and treat this leading cause of death. Over the last 45 years the Heart Foundation has invested more than $160 million in lifesaving research. We are the leading non-government funder of cardiovascular research in Australia.
- **Using information:** the Heart Foundation reviews international and local research to develop guidelines and educational programs for health professionals to improve treatment and management of heart disease so Australians receive the best care available.
- **Supporting individuals and families:** the Heart Foundation's national telephone information service Heartline 1300 36 27 87 receives almost 70,000 calls for help on heart health issues each year. We also distribute 1.7 million publications nationwide and have more than 400,000 unique visitors to our Heartsite www.heartfoundation.com.au each year.
- **Through community action:** from local walking groups to healthy eating programs for school canteens, the Heart Foundation has developed health programs to improve heart health and save lives in local communities.

As an independent, Australia-wide charity, the Heart Foundation receives minimal government funding so we rely on generous donations, sales and gifts in wills from individual Australians as well as sponsorship and donations from companies in order to continue our life-saving work.

Heartsite www.heartfoundation.com.au

Heartline 1300 36 27 87